I0797944

BUY YOURSELF THE DAMN *flowers*

BUY YOURSELF THE DAMN *flowers*

The *self-love* guide to growing, healing and learning to put *yourself* first

Tam Kaur

Lagom

First published in the UK by Lagom
An imprint of Bonnier Books UK
5th Floor, HYLO, 105 Bunhill Row,
London, EC1Y 8LZ

A CIP catalogue record for this book is available from the British Library.

Hardback ISBN: 9781785121746

Also available as an ebook and an audiobook

7 9 10 8

Design and Typeset by Envy Design Ltd
Illustrations © Shutterstock
Printed and bound in Great Britain by Clays Ltd, Elcograf S.p.A.

The authorised representative in the EEA is
Bonnier Books UK (Ireland) Limited.
Registered office address: Block B, The Crescent Building
Northwood, Santry
Dublin 9, D09 C6X8, Ireland
compliance@bonnierbooks.ie

www.bonnierbooks.co.uk

Dedicated to my past heartaches.

Thank you for the pain and the lessons.

I found the light within myself in the healing process.

CONTENTS

INTRODUCTION

The story of how self-love saved me

I have been a hopeless romantic for as long as I can remember. I immersed myself in love stories, movies and fantasies, even as a child. From *Cinderella* to *Veer-Zaara,* I placed myself in every romantic narrative, dreaming of the day I'd find a Prince Charming to wait 22 years, run through an airport, kiss me in the rain, publicly declare their love for me and hold a boombox outside my bedroom window. Call me crazy, but I believed it would happen.

Throughout my teenage years, all I wanted was to be in a relationship, and shortly after turning 17 years old, I got just that. I was taken out on dates, I was surprised with an abnormally large teddy bear on Valentine's Day, I received romantic text messages every day – and all this affection led me to ignore the fact that my boyfriend . . . was still very much in love with his ex. It was obvious in how he would find ways to bring her up in most of our conversations and was absolutely outraged when he found out she had moved on to someone else. I spent a lot of my time feeling insecure and comparing myself to the ex. I would regularly look at her Instagram, trying to figure out what I was doing wrong. It took a few scrolls to discover they had everything in common that we didn't.

What hurt most of all was that his ex and I looked nothing alike. Was I not his type? She was petite, curvy and feminine; he casually reminded me I was too tall, too skinny and had shoulders that were too wide. I would occasionally slip away from the present to imagine what they would've spoken about . . . Why hadn't he unfollowed her yet? What made her so interesting? Was he still messaging her while being with me?

The few friends I confided in about this problem reassured me by laughing off my concerns. 'She's got nothing on you!' and 'You're so much prettier!' they'd exclaim. I wanted to believe them, and I tried, but nothing worked. I had this deep pit in my stomach and a voice that screamed 'YOU'LL NEVER BE ENOUGH FOR HIM'. So I did what any insecure 17-year-old would do – I chased his validation.

Suddenly, only his opinion mattered. I wanted him to *see* me, to be *with* me and, most importantly, to be *in love* with me. So, throughout our four-month relationship, I wore more makeup, dressed in a way I thought he would like, played the 'easy-going girlfriend', gave him my undivided attention and pretended to be interested in all his hobbies. I thought it was working and that he had moved on from his ex, until one day my best friend confirmed the worst – my first ever boyfriend had confided in a mutual friend that he 'preferred' his ex to me. My world shattered. Was I not good enough?

I immediately called him to confront him, hoping it was a misunderstanding. After a few pitiable attempts to lie, he admitted what he said to his friend. He couldn't bring himself to deny the love he still had for his ex. As soon as I realised that I could never live up to the idea of her in his head, I begrudgingly ended it.

I had spent so many years fixated on the idea of having a boyfriend that I was thrilled just to have somebody who said they loved me, even if they didn't mean it. Only, it wasn't just that. I had spent my teen years hiding myself away so much that even at the age of 17, I didn't know who I was. I had always been painfully shy, socially awkward and extremely self-doubting. I didn't want anybody to look at me or talk to me, but I was so desperate to be pretty and liked. And yet *I* didn't like who I was. Every day I went to school and I compared myself to everyone around me, especially the girls who always seemed so effortlessly put together. No matter how hard I tried, how many YouTube makeup tutorials I watched or new clothes I bought, it never gave me the confidence they exuded. If somebody asked me what I admired about myself, I'd be lost for words. I ended up in this situation because I never took the time to learn and appreciate who I am and what I really want out of life. Unfortunately, I spent the following years refusing to do so . . .

Shortly after my first relationship, I found myself consumed by a tumultuous love for a narcissist. I was immediately swept off my feet due to his love-bombing (extreme over-affection as soon as you meet) tactics. I fell for it so easily because no one had paid attention to me like that before. No one had claimed I was the prettiest girl in the world with such conviction and no one had texted me essays of their admiration for my personality. I had never thought of myself fondly before, so this attention felt comforting. The narcissist alternated giant gestures of adoration with threats, control, manipulation and emotional abuse (not that I knew it at the time). And I still stayed. Why? Because when it was good, our love felt like a movie – much like those I watched as a child. He wrote poems for me, he whisked me away for romantic getaways, he sent me lyrics that reminded him of our love, he understood my favourite film references, he'd greet me with fresh red roses and I would never have to ask him for anything because he would have already done it. It didn't matter that I'd quietly cry myself to sleep after our recurring 3am arguments. I was so grateful to have found someone who expressed their care for me so passionately that I felt I had to cling onto it, because for a girl like me, a love like this doesn't come so easy.

I held even tighter when he told me I couldn't wear dresses, belittled me in public or shamed me for feeling upset. I had put the narcissist on a pedestal and this was reassuring for my self-worth. I'd never imagined I could attract someone so effortlessly cool and stylish. Women threw themselves at him, yet he chose me. Girls at my school praised his appearance and it satisfied the validation I had desired for years. But because I placed all my worth in him, in something outside myself, I was trapped in this abusive relationship far beyond the point at which we broke up.

In the three months after the relationship ended, I threw myself into excessive partying, drinking and shameless flirting. All while speaking to my ex whenever he felt like it and dreaming that we'd be together again. At this point, I had just started university. It was my chance at a fresh start, a new me and better opportunities, all of which I dismissed to pursue attention from someone who didn't really care about me. But my mind was filled with chasing temporary happiness and external fulfilment rather than facing my biggest demon – myself.

We broke up shortly after I started university. My newfound freedom and friends became a never-ending argument, which influenced the narcissist to dismiss our year-long love in a single text message. It broke me. I was left a shell of a person who would stop at nothing to get him back. Finally, though, in our period of on-and-off dating, I could see our relationship for what it was and accept that my life felt much more peaceful without him in it.

I started researching toxic relationships online and discovered the term 'narcissism' for the very first time. After a brief reading of the signs and behaviours, I realised that the perception of my 'true love' I had held onto for so long was nothing short of an illusion. There was nothing left to justify or deny when every manipulation and threat was explained so clearly on the screen in front of me. So, I left the narcissist for good on New Year's Day, a year and a half after we first got together, and in the process of trying to piece my heart back together, I found somebody else. Somebody who was nice to me and conveyed nothing but pure innocence. It felt like the safe space I needed, yet I was deciding to settle because I hadn't healed from the trauma of my last relationship.

The truth is, I could only wrap my head around the break-up if I could find someone to fill his space. After all, how could I be single?! It's not like I could go about my days contentedly, not thinking about when someone would save me from myself.

Plus, I had a point to prove. How could I have been so stupid as to have pined after a toxic relationship for so long? All my loved ones begged me not to go back and I had ignored them. Every. Single. Time. 'They just don't get it,' I'd say to reassure myself. In the aftermath, I realised I was wrong all along and that was a pain I wasn't brave enough to face. I had to prove I was mature enough for a healthy love and that what had happened to me in the past was not my fault.

So, I finally found a secure relationship. I was in denial throughout, convincing myself I loved this person and I could build a happy life with him. But without fail, every night, I'd lay awake beside him, staring at the ceiling, wondering if the narcissist was thinking of me. I tried to push the feeling away, to keep re-reading the 'cons' list I had written about him in the notes app on my iPhone. Nostalgia was my worst enemy, creating a montage of our best memories while minimising the bad. At this point, I wasn't aware that narcissistic heartbreaks cannot be dealt with the same. Still, I poured so much into trying to make this new relationship work, offering romantic gestures, always doing things his way, spending every single moment with him. It was good, I was getting there. I even brought him home to meet my family. Everyone loved us as a couple. *Maybe this will work after all*, I thought.

Then, lockdown hit. I moved back home from university and used the abundance of free time to start working on my passions and career while making the relationship work from a distance. But, inevitably, this life-changing event prompted a lot of self-reflection. I spent a lot of my time alone. So I started the practice of journaling every evening, which made my aspirations for life much clearer, but it also forced me to confront my delusions. I'd find myself writing about everything I wanted for my life and my partner never appeared in those plans. I also read self-development books and watched videos on how to progress in my dream job as a content creator. This finally reignited the spark that I had lost while seeking men over the years, and I had to recognise that I wasn't happy in this relationship. Something didn't have to go terribly wrong for me to justify why this wasn't the right place for me to be. I decided to leave this relationship and focus on building a better life for myself over the summer. I could do this now. I had never experienced the desire to stay single before . . . was this a turning point?

It started off promisingly, with more time committed to seeing my loved ones while working hard on building my dream life. I fell in love with the process of developing my craft as a video creator, forming new daily routines, journaling to meet my highest self and focusing more on building more aligned friendships. Life felt thrilling again. I really thought that this could be the start of a new me. The girl who achieves all her goals, makes her family proud and gains true independence. But it came crashing down when my friend casually mentioned that this guy who we knew was interested in me. Except this wasn't just any guy, it was THE guy from our high school. Your clichéd confident, popular, arrogant-but-lovable, attends every party, wouldn't-take-a-second-look-at-you type of guy. The kind of guy you admire from afar but don't think too much about because you know you'd never have a chance. Well, that guy texted me. I stared at the first message in shock, my teenage self's warped self-image shrieking in astonishment. I casually sent a text back, reassuring myself it would just be a summer romance; I've promised myself too much after all.

Once again, I refused to take a real look at myself. I spent the summer months distracting myself with vision boards, late-night work and hours at the gym instead of confronting my deep-rooted discomfort with myself. Of course, I pined for more dates with the cliché high school boy; it inflated my ego and numbed my insecurities for a while, so I prioritised prolonging that feeling. I was addicted to running farther away from my younger self instead of accepting and loving her for all her oddities. This dating experience was like a huge neon sign in my head reading 'you're *prettier* now, you're *enviable*, guys put *you* on the pedestal' and that's all the validation I thought I needed.

Autumn rolled around and my summer romance was suddenly a very real relationship. At the time, I thought I was head-over-heels in love. In reality, I was practically playing tug-of-war for affection with an emotionally unavailable man. Our days consisted of me pleading with him to plan a date, hold my hand, take my picture, express his feelings, stay engaged in our conversations or reciprocate so much as a compliment. He always promised to change but nothing happened. So we took a break and while my heart ached in his absence, he instantly followed his ex back, along with a dozen other girls.

That was the moment I could no longer deny that this person had never loved me. I got so caught up in waiting for him to show that he cared, but I was waiting for something that would never arrive. This hit my ego harder than the others due to the constant back and forth. He never deemed me worthy enough of any effort, and then moved on straight away, which made me feel overwhelmingly unlovable. That was my breaking point. There were no more tears left to fall. I was left experiencing an all-consuming rage running through my body instead, and I sat on my bedroom floor alone at midnight with no one to take it out on.

As I stared at my mascara-stained face in the mirrored wall opposite me, I swore I would never allow myself to encounter such treatment ever again. I made myself a promise to focus on myself for one whole year, to stop dating completely and to learn to love myself so unconditionally that I would never compromise my standards just to have company. No more self-hate, pity or shame. I didn't know how I was going to do it, but I knew the fire in my belly would get me there.

I know what you're thinking . . . *Four back-to-back relationships in the space of two years, an inability to stay single and extremely low standards?!* All true. But honestly, I'm glad I met each of those men. Those relationships formed the start of my beautiful story of transformation and journey to self-discovery. I truly believe that it just *had* to happen that way for me. In the end, I realised I was always trying to be good enough for other people to love me and it only resulted in me drifting further away from my true self. Whereas actually, if I had spent some time focusing on being good enough for *myself*, the self-love would have allowed me to experience the care that I deserved AND prevented all the pain and heartbreak.

Three years later, I still implement all the practices I learned along the way and my self-perception, detachment and self-worth have never been more unbreakable.

I have now reached a paradise where I inspire over 1,000,000 people online to master confidence, date themselves and give the love they crave back to themselves. I can't remember the last time I didn't feel enough in a room full of other beautiful people. I regularly spend time alone eating in restaurants and embarking on new life experiences. I made my dreams my number one focus and achieved everything on my vision board as a result. My newfound confidence has allowed me to attract like-minded company and build friendships with the people I used to look up to. Most importantly, I have never felt stronger. I no longer look at the past in shame; I have healed to the point that I embrace every adversity that is thrown at me. I love every mistake I made, how I've handled it, how I've grown from it and what I've done to get to where I am right now.

In this book, I will teach you how to achieve a self-love mindset, validate yourself and never settle or spend years chasing others just as I once did. This self-love guide is split into three parts – understanding, healing and reawakening. Part one, 'Understanding', contains chapters on breaking down the real meaning of self-love, managing misconceptions and learning how to practise it on your new journey. Part two, 'Healing', is centred on coping with the challenges you will face when learning how to love yourself unconditionally and dealing healthily with the wounds that may hold you back from doing so. Lastly, part three, 'Reawakening' focuses on the new life you will live after you've let go of your past and developed a stronger relationship with yourself.

Your newfound self-love will influence how you show up in

all parts of your life and how you navigate certain situations. In every part, I will break down the definition of each concept while challenging the limiting beliefs you may hold about them. I will explain what to do, while including various ideas and examples throughout to make this new belief system practical and memorable.

At the end of every chapter there is a chapter summary and a chapter homework. The summaries will refresh your memory on the practice of self-love as you revisit this book at various stages of your life, and the homework provides actionable steps that allow you to put everything you've learned into practice . . . so your time spent reading leads to *real growth*.

I started this journey as a hopeless romantic, seeing my singlehood as a punishment as I constantly awaited the love that would 'save me'. I finally provided myself with everything I was looking for, and I believe that you too can soon get to the point of your journey where you realise that you are the love of your own life.

PART ONE:

UNDERSTANDING

Everything you've ever questioned about self-love answered

CHAPTER 1:

EVERYTHING YOU'VE BEEN TAUGHT ABOUT SELF-LOVE IS INCORRECT

What does loving yourself really mean?

I had always associated self-love with the surface-level meaning of self-care I had in my head – face masks, getting dressed up and buying expensive beauty products. I never took a second look at the concept and just assumed it was one of those overused inspirational Instagram quotes. I never really understood it and I was quite sceptical of the notion. After all, I'd always look in the mirror and assure myself I was confident and loved, but that didn't stop me tolerating low-value experiences from my long list of exes.

If you look up self-love in the dictionary, you will be faced with the definition 'regard for one's own well-being and happiness'. If you search online, you will be met with an abundance of articles which highlight self-care habits like taking a bubble bath or spending time with your loved ones. To me, self-love is much more than that. So, here's a list of the actual components of self-love that will allow you real understanding of this concept, which is the first step to introducing this practice into your life. Below, I have compiled these components I have discovered over the years while on my journey of self-love, combining them with my own lessons.

THE 10 COMPONENTS OF REAL SELF-LOVE

1. The five love languages

How often do you give affection to yourself and fill your own cup? Probably not as often as the care you give to everyone else, so let's change that. The five love languages were identified by American author Gary Chapman in his book, *The Five Love Languages: How to Express Heartfelt Commitment to Your Mate.* There is a popular test that uncovers your desired emotional fulfilment. It is believed that one 'language' always stands out in making us feel the most loved, even without the others present. Although this was designed for couples, it's actually a great way to understand yourself and your needs on a deeper level, and forms the perfect foundation when starting your self-love practices. You can take the test online (https://5lovelanguages.com/quizzes/love-language) and once you have your result, your job is to give your love language back to yourself. These are the five love languages and why they might be important to you . . .

Quality time: You value undivided attention, deep conversations, feeling prioritised and engaging in meaningful activities. For someone to make time for you while balancing a demanding schedule is a much more beautiful act of love to you than spending money or expressing compliments. You might prioritise looking after others, impressing your boss or being the fun, easy-going friend.

A close friend half listening while scrolling on Instagram or continuous rescheduled plans can make you feel undervalued – this is your hurt language.

For your self-love language, you need to start taking that time for yourself. It's easy to get swept up in daily life, errands, obligations, work, but how often do you prioritise doing things you enjoy? Here are some ideas: make reservations for dinner dates alone, take a 30-plus-minute walk to soak up nature and listen to the birds chirping, spend an entire evening painting for fun, solo travel for a whole weekend, meditate as soon as you wake up to ease peacefully into your busy day and, finally, take a break from everything to do *nothing* for the day.

When we put work and errands first, we are showing ourselves that we are not a priority in our own lives. As uncomfortable as it might feel to begin with, spending time alone regularly makes everything in life clearer – you are more connected to yourself and what you really want. Your happiness becomes a priority and thus your mental health is already on the mend. In a study done at the University of Reading, researchers found that adults whose solitude was down to personal choice experienced less stress and were more confident in their authenticity. So it is only when we can sit alone with our own thoughts that we can truly grow as individuals and understand ourselves. If you don't know yourself fully, how could you ever love yourself?

Words of affirmation: You like to feel empowered, appreciated and uplifted. You value people communicating their appreciation towards you and, as a result, a simple 'I'm so proud of you' can make your day.

When someone speaks to you harshly or is over-critical of you, it represents your hurt language.

For this language type, it's important to take care of the treatment you are prepared to accept from others and from yourself. You can start practising recognition by writing a letter to your future self. Think of this as an opportunity to transport yourself through time. What do you hope you've achieved by then? What do you think your older self would miss about your current life? What do you hope your future self never forgets about herself? What reminders can you give her today to show her you'll always be rooting for her?

Another way to practise this love language is by celebrating yourself in the way you usually would others. After all, we usually give the love we so deeply crave, so it's time for us to actually make it happen for ourselves. Journaling is the easiest way to affirm your self-love. Write a detailed entry about a time you were proud of yourself. How was it when you got there? Why did this grow your confidence? What did overcoming your self-doubts look like? To make this a weekly habit, you can simply write down what you did well at the end of every week to acknowledge your accomplishments.

Complimenting yourself should never be reserved for the big fancy milestones in life. You are entitled to praise at any point of any day. Just the habit of speaking kinder words to yourself daily can change your life for the better. We often don't realise the harsh language we use to speak to ourselves when all we have done is make a simple mistake. Over time, our self-talk builds the self-perception we're stuck with and can be the difference between a strong foundation of confidence or depending on external validation to feel good about ourselves. Imagine how good life will feel when you become your own cheerleader.

Gift giving: Giving presents is the most passionate expression of love in your eyes. The process of learning about a loved one is expressed in figuring out what would add the most value in their life. Seeing their face light up when you've treated them to something and thus showing that they're present in your mind is a major way you show love.

However, being given a gift with minimal consideration for your desires, someone forgetting a special occasion or simply dismissing the idea of giving a bouquet of flowers you walked past in the grocery store is your hurt language.

So, when was the last time you splurged on something for yourself? I'm sure you've lost count of the number of times you added something to your wish list but never allocated the time or resources to get it. We can get so wrapped up in the game of saving that we never grant a budget purely for our pleasure. You work hard, you try your best every day, you've fought and conquered every problem life has thrown your way, and yet you feel guilty for spending £5 on a festive latte from your favourite coffee shop. Life is for enjoyment, so commit to giving yourself a gift, whether it be in the form of a coffee, a new lipstick or a red velvet cupcake from your local supermarket.

Studies into the psychology behind treating yourself have shown that it helps you to regain a sense of control over your life, while simultaneously feeling happier, cared for and more confident. This isn't exclusive to spending money, but can be achieved through giving yourself the day off or baking your favourite dessert. When you put everybody or everything else first, you are constantly reinforcing the idea that you have not done enough to earn those small gifts of self-pleasure. But remember, you are always enough.

Physical touch: Hugs, hand holding, cuddles, kisses and any other form of physical affection make you feel connected. Just a gentle stroke from a loved one while sitting in silence can make you feel wanted. This is because touching causes the brain to release the bonding hormone oxytocin as well as relieving stress and anxiety.

It is often assumed that this love language is only possible to receive from another person but, once again, being alone does not mean you will go without. Hiding yourself away from the world, others being distant or cold or attaching to the idea that you will only feel connected with a partner by your side is you living out your hurt language.

Committing to your singlehood for a while should never equal isolation or a deprivation of physical closeness. Once you master the art of going to bed wrapped up in a fresh duvet and cuddling your favourite pillow, blissfully drifting off to sleep without wishing someone was by your side, you'll find peace in the fact that you are complete and loved as you are on your own. When the time is right, you will allow the person who actually deserves to hold you at night into your life. But until then, you are capable of fulfilling all of your desires.

Alternatively, you can book yourself a massage, get a facial, invest in your bedsheets, use a weighted blanket, buy a vibrator, book in for a mani-pedi or do yoga. This will still gift you those same feelings of love released by our love and happiness hormones.

Acts of service: You treasure feeling looked after. Just the thoughtfulness of someone helping with a chore, going out of their way to reduce your workload or accompanying you on a task to make it more enjoyable means the world. This is all about the experience of feeling looked after and provided for. Someone is showing they care for you through their actions of trying to make your life easier, and that's the most generous act of all in your eyes. On the flip side, someone neglecting your needs or showing disinterest in contributing to your life can make you feel rejected.

Acts of service is a wonderful self-love language that will also aid your independence and productivity in all areas of life. Blocking out every Sunday morning to complete your chores and meal plan, ahead of a new week, is a great way to remove any potential stress for yourself. It's about identifying where you often struggle and actioning a system which creates a more pleasant flow through your days. When you are waiting to be saved by somebody else or anticipating reaching the 'right time' when things will 'finally be better', you are consigning your present moment to a constant state of suffering instead of taking responsibility for your routine. So, can you reorganise your space, keep your calendar updated, tick off your to-do list or start habit stacking to free up more time to do the things you enjoy most? After all, this practice is all about ease and fulfilment.

I discovered the concept of love languages in my teens and fell in love with the idea, as it made so much sense to me. I've repeated the test many times and 'quality time' always comes out on top for me. This didn't come as a surprise – it didn't matter how much affection somebody showed me, if they weren't initiating deep conversation in order to understand me more and actually see me for me, I'd feel completely alone in the relationship.

So, when I quit dating and started spending time alone, my first instinct was to dine at a restaurant by myself. Absolutely terrifying and awkward I know, but that's what I really liked doing with others, so I gave it back to myself. I'd sit patiently after ordering my food, people watching and staying present with my thoughts. I'd savour every bite of my favourite meal and have little conversations with myself in my head. It was therapeutic. I was checking in with myself. I knew everything that was going on in my life, so I had all the right questions. It prompted deeper thought about my life and what I wanted from it.

2. Self-acceptance

This is all about fully accepting your strengths, weaknesses and everything in between. As author Mark Twain put it 'the worst loneliness is to not be comfortable with yourself'.

To master self-acceptance, you must reach a state of mind

where you understand that nothing about you is either 'good' nor 'bad'. You are a work in progress, sure, so there are attributes you might love and others you feel you'd like to work on. But, overall, this is the act of loving yourself without *having* to make any changes.

As integral as adapting and evolving throughout life is, it should never be our answer to making peace with ourselves. Relying on a full face of makeup, losing weight, making a lot of money, owning a big house, eating healthily, winning awards or being admired to feel worthy might only be a temporary fix that will keep you in a cycle of chasing the next best thing. You must love yourself *unconditionally* or else you give your power away, allowing others to tell you when and whether you are worthy.

If you base your self-worth on accomplishments and titles then the second you miss a gym session or lose a job or relationship, all your self-love slips away with it. There is nothing you need to have to be worthy of love. Where do we get these ideas of what we must do in order to be 'normal'? Because our friends are doing it? Because those are our parents' expectations? Because that's society's idea of living successfully? When did any of those people live your unique path from your individual perspective? Where did those people get their idea of normal? Was it not just another notion passed down by another who couldn't see the importance in contrariety? You are beautiful, lovable and full of potential, with every one of your idiosyncrasies.

We are so consumed with the idea of what we are *supposed* to be that it holds us back from seeing our true form in all its beauty. You were born with a unique viewpoint, yet you assume it's incorrect when it doesn't match your peers'. You have a creative flair that is ready to inspire a stranger on the street, yet you rely on the latest trends to build your outfit every morning. You have the answer to every possible problem you could ever encounter in life, yet you ignore your intuition to ask for advice before every decision you make. So, sit with the discomfort of yourself and understand that the phases when you feel sad, broken and lazy do not make you any harder to love, they make you human and vulnerable. Self-acceptance begins with trusting oneself and ceasing to prioritise the opinions of others.

3. Self-sufficiency

Independence, the ability to provide for oneself without the aid of others, is a core pillar of self-love because once you can survive and thrive alone, you'll never be stuck with someone's mistreatment of you due to your fear of being alone. Once you remove dependence from your life, you make space for company that exceeds every standard you've ever set. Learning how to be happy on your own and fulfil all your needs allows you the freedom to choose who you want to be with. Plus, it is an essential skill heightening your confidence and removing any self-doubt.

Every time you take on the challenge of completing a task you're unsure of, you prove to yourself that you're smarter than you give yourself credit for, you're more resilient, you're more resourceful than you ever thought. When you are uncomfortable with handling things by yourself, remind yourself of every battle you've fought through, every piece you've picked up when relationships broke, every time you woke up to fight another day, despite how you felt. But when you feel frustrated with your solitude and you long to have someone by your side, you are simultaneously disregarding every piece of joy you have been responsible for in your life and your potential. So start achieving alone, whether it be cooking all your meals, learning DIY, taking driving lessons, improving your financial literacy or setting up a business.

This is another example of the acts of service love language – we are putting our needs first and taking the time to remove the pain from our lives so we can live with minimal tension without waiting for someone else to come along and fix it for us.

4. Self-discovery

This is the act of learning entirely about oneself. Wholly understanding who you are at your core is a severely underrated skill. What fills you up? What could you not live without? What makes you feel loved? What feels comfortable? What scares you? What do you cry about at night? What parts of yourself do you hide away? Do you prioritise others over yourself? Who makes you feel understood and why? How do you pick yourself up after a bad day? What emotions arise when it's your birthday? What do your good days have in common? Take the time to recognise your TRUE self.

Your true self is the person you are when you have the entire house to yourself, when you're not worrying about how you look, when you let your goofy side out with your friends. Not the masked self you present to the world when you change your outfit last minute out of fear of being overdressed or speak a different way when meeting new people to appear more likeable.

Understanding who you really are and where your heart lies will grant you peace and remove the need to seek understanding from others, because now you can reassure yourself on a daily basis. In my own journey to discovering my authenticity, I completely eradicated the need to be perceived as 'cool', as, in doing so, I had been limiting my expression and opinions. The more I learned about myself, the more I realised how outspoken, loud, passionately aggressive, childish and enthusiastic I was. Leaning into that energy made me respect myself more because I was following my instincts rather than questioning how each action would be perceived and how I would be defined by everybody else.

After all, every single person you know views you differently, through their own lens, which is altered by their individual life experiences, trauma and mindsets. YOU are the only one who's been by your side your entire life. You know every trial and tribulation you've been through. No one can ever compete with that – not your parents, not your sibling, not your childhood best friend. You will know yourself more than anybody else could even try to. But it must be your choice to hone that gift and develop it as time goes on.

5. Solo dating

Solo dating is the act of giving yourself every experience you would usually wait to receive in a relationship. It's learning to enjoy your own company without seeking support from anyone else.

That's right – you need to take yourself out to movies, compliment yourself and buy *yourself* the damn flowers. This boosts your self-esteem, builds up your confidence and grows your independence, which are all important pillars before eventually dating another person.

You can solo date whether you're single or in a relationship. This is crucial in taking time for yourself for leisure, experiencing the world without having to wait around for others, being alone with your thoughts and understanding yourself. Don't think that other people have to be with you for you to experience life; do your favourite activities regardless of everyone else's busy schedules. This is important because once you make it a habit to provide yourself with every form of love you would usually expect from others, alongside finally feeling content with your alone time, you will be protected from chasing bare minimum experiences ever again just for the sake of wanting company.

Gone will be the days of making excuses for your partner's emotional absence or lack of romance. You'll already give yourself the most passionate expression of love and, as a result, your eyes won't wander twice towards someone who won't match that and then double it. Loneliness isn't this scary state of living which we should avoid, but rather a gift to be embraced. Get comfortable with your solitude because you never know how much time you have left to enjoy it. One day you will meet your soulmate (hell, it could be tomorrow) and as wonderful as that life will be, you will reminisce about the days when life only revolved around you, when you could do anything at any moment without having to consider someone else.

You are your own greatest companion. Enjoy the benefits of being selfish and doing everything you desire to create your dream reality. This will prepare you for the healthiest relationship full of boundaries, a love that can be felt and a strong sense of self.

6. Boundaries

Creating boundaries means drawing a line between us and the limits we set for our lives to define the appropriate behaviour we accept within our relationships. Certified relationship coach Kate Mangona states that boundaries are for our own emotional safety, it's never about punishing the other person.

You have every right to say no, to put yourself first, to skip the party and to do whatever it takes to maintain your energy and emotional balance. People pleasing is the fastest way to surrender your self-respect. When you feel afraid to say no, over-compensate, chase approval and prioritise others' time over yours, you are telling yourself that you are unimportant and other people hold more value in your life than you do. By continuing to engage in this practice, you are only developing a fear of rejection, co-dependency and low self-esteem. Not only this, but you are now more attractive to narcissists and energy vampires.

Your life mirrors your perception and thoughts about yourself. When you feel insecure and unworthy, you will attract partners who treat you as such because they feel superior to you. When you feel like you should silence your voice to validate others' experience, you attract friends who expect you to solve all their problems and who never give you enough consideration.

When you do anything to be liked, you will attract people who take advantage of your kindness and treat you like a doormat.

Boundary setting isn't as intimidating as it seems. It starts with a regular, polite conversation: 'I would appreciate it if you didn't comment on my weight anymore' or 'It hurts my feelings when you disregard my presence' and so on (further examples on implementing boundary setting will be explored in Chapter 10). Regularly communicate your limits and preferences with people and prepare to cut out those who choose to disrespect your needs. Giving love at the expense of your feelings is not love, it is hatred towards yourself. When you can recognise what you will and will not accept from the people in your life and then raise it when necessary, you can finally feel secure in your own body again because you are always protecting your best interests. Once you grow this healthy bond with yourself, the relationships in your life will look the same. People only treat you how you treat yourself.

7. Mental health

Taking care of one's emotional, psychological and social wellbeing must be prioritised above all else – your job, your partner, your friends, your commitments, even your family. Research shows that 'rates of probable mental disorders have increased since 2017. In 2020, one in six (16 per cent) children aged 5 to 16 years were identified as having a probable mental disorder'. Mental health and self-love go hand in hand. It's about making sure everything inside us is functioning at its absolute best so that our output matches our potential. Consistently contributing to your mental health motivates more positive behaviour, like strong boundaries, better discipline and improved relationships. This is because good mental health lowers our anxiety and stress, improving our ability to show up for ourselves and others as a result. Think about it: when you put other people and work commitments above your sleep, personal time and leisure, you are sabotaging your ability to achieve and live the life you truly want. When you scroll on social media for hours on end, you are volunteering to obsess over strangers instead of cultivating a happy life.

Change your perspective and the way you view the world – don't go to the gym to lose weight, go to the gym to hack your happy hormones, to chase that feeling of accomplishment when you walk out, to regulate your mood so you always feel your best. Don't scroll online endlessly to feel social, call up a friend and have a conversation to connect and stimulate your love hormones. It's about making healthy choices today so that you can have a better tomorrow.

You should never feel guilty for being selfish when your mental health is in a bad place. Protect it at all costs. Take the space if you need it. Stay home if you don't want to attend the event. Turn off your phone if you don't have the capacity to respond. It's okay. We all have bad mental health days, so even if it only lasts 24 hours, take the time to self-soothe and be extra gentle with yourself. Do what you enjoy, whether that's watching your favourite comfort movie, reading a book, going on a walk or going for lunch with a friend; you *deserve* days like this. Maintaining good mental health trumps everything else and is an important part of self-love.

8. Inner monologue

This is how you speak to yourself in your mind. You know that voice in your head that occasionally tells you that you're not good enough? This is what we call our inner critic, your very own built-in bully, and it is your responsibility to silence it. Using your own voice to inflict judgement and criticism on yourself is often the result of a distorted self-perception built on low self-esteem. This can be easily identified when it expresses a hurtful attitude towards us, demeans our character or makes fun of our behaviour with statements like 'no one cares that you're here', 'but what if you fail?', 'that was so embarrassing', etc. Manifestation expert Roxie Nafousi says 'become aware of your inner critic. When you hear it speak, take a moment to pause and choose a new thought to replace it. It will feel uncomfortable at first but with practice it will really help you to build self-esteem.'

You must learn to navigate the voice of your inner critic because it will be with you throughout your lifetime. You can remove its authority by introducing your inner companion. Every time your inner critic is about to shame you, respond with self-compassion, bringing out your inner companion thoughts. For example, 'You're so irresponsible for staying in bed for that long' (inner critic) turns into 'You listened to your body's desires and got to have some extra rest! Tomorrow is another chance to try again with your early riser goal.' You get to decide the narrative of your life and it can be anything you dream of (inner companion).

Don't surrender space for your inner critic to control your confidence and emotions. Thoughts aren't real; you can let them pass by and you even have the power to change them over time using the inner companion method. This is focused on practising responding to yourself with kindness every day until it becomes a habit. Never underestimate the importance of positive self-talk – it is the first step in successfully manifesting, reducing stress, achieving your goals, improving your mental health and cultivating self-love.

9. Inner child

Your inner child is a representation of your younger self and your childhood memories. It's like imagining the six- or seven-year-old version of yourself sat before you. You can see her, hear her, talk to her and, most importantly, understand her. What does she need right now? How could she be loved more? How is she feeling? Where is her safe space? Who are you to her? Her protector, guider, parent? We all require re-parenting in one way or another. Although our parents did the best they could with the resources and energy they had at the time, most of us have unresolved internal conflicts, trauma and a skewed self-image. When you can start viewing your child self so clearly, you can get into her mind and understand what will truly fill her cup. The easiest way to start this is with language.

Your self-love gets knocked down every time you start criticising yourself subconsciously, when you doubt whether you can achieve your goals, or point out which parts of your appearance you despise, or convince yourself that no one really likes you. Now imagine you're saying all of those things to that seven-year-old version of yourself stood innocently beside you, gazing up at you in admiration. She does not deserve to be spoken to that way and neither do you.

This is the quickest way to have more compassion for yourself, which is the foundation of self-love. Your younger self carries so much unconditional love for who you are and who you will grow to be; when you remember that love, hope and goodness you carry, you'll only accept experiences that align with those qualities. You'll know that you deserve more and that your child self is counting on you. Plus, who dreams bigger and with more certainty than children? When you reconnect with that self-belief you once had, your confidence in your abilities will finally match the life you really deserve.

10. Authenticity and confidence

In a digital age where we are exposed to others' experiences, clothes, habits, behaviours and opinions more than ever, it can be a struggle to stay true to our genuine character and beliefs rather than conforming to societal expectations and ideals, partly due to an imposed need to be accepted on social media. Although following trends, agreeing with the majority and trying to fit in might seem like a safe space in which to reside, it is actually a trap that will slowly make you lose your identity and feel unworthy.

So, question yourself: why do I always ask for a second opinion when I'm about to make a life decision, post something online, buy a dress or choose a new hairstyle? Why isn't my opinion enough? Why don't I trust myself? Trust is the key to self-love and confidence. Every time you feel tempted to ask someone for reassurance on an action you are about to take, remember this: you are the only person who has experienced every single thought in your head, battled every adversity thrown at you and lived through every second of your life – so how could someone else possibly even begin to conjure up a valid opinion on your life? They cannot. Their opinion is merely an accumulation of their own lessons, experiences and traumas, all of which make up their reality, not yours.

Once you realise this, every single opinion or disagreement loses all significance and instead you understand that you are fully equipped to live out your own life, regardless of anyone's thoughts on how you do it. Even if you hide away your quirks and perfect the mask you show to the world, you will still be judged because people look at things through their own lens of beliefs, rather than the knowledge they have about you (which we now know is very little).

So, wouldn't you rather be your true, weird, one-of-a-kind self and, in the process, develop a numbness to the judgement rather than being a prisoner to the unlikely chance that a complete stranger might just be thinking about you? Not to mention you are doing yourself a huge favour by being yourself. You attract real friends and more aligned opportunities, and you filter out what doesn't serve you. Self-love is dressing for yourself instead of the occasion, posting what you like, not what will impress others, speaking your mind at the dinner table and expressing yourself in whichever way you like at whatever moment you wish.

When beginning to implement these 10 components, it's important to start with the one that directly impacts your biggest struggle when it comes to self-love. For example, my desire to date and pour love into relationships held me back from myself because of my inability to be alone. So I started with solo dating because it replaced the need to find somebody else to show up for me in this way. By addressing this first, I stayed consistent on my path of solitude much faster. I worked through all other nine practices, some which were more challenging to me than others – for example, while inner child work came pretty naturally to me, I still find myself having to be consciously aware of the way I prioritise my mental health. I remind myself that self-love is not a 'quick fix' achieved by simply learning the 10 components, but rather an ongoing journey.

SELF-LOVE MYTHS DEBUNKED

There are a plethora of misconceptions floating around the internet as to what self-love actually means, and this is part of the reason why so many of us fail to carry out this practice in our lives. Often, it associated with narcissism, due to society's unfamiliarity with openly expressing self-admiration because insecurities seem to be more common and acceptable. Other times, it's labelled as a 'coping strategy' strictly for singles, and the majority of the time, it's restricted to aesthetic self-care habits. Only when you learn these differences, will you be able to confidently and successfully fall in love with yourself . . .

Self-love vs narcissism

An insecure society is easier to control. We have been conditioned to believe that having a high self-importance and being obsessed with yourself is narcissistic and selfish. We're taught to value being 'humble', the definition of which is to have a low sense of one's own importance. The truth is that most people don't want to see you thrive and a lot of them are threatened by confidence and certainty. So, people with those qualities are labelled as 'vain' and 'full of themselves'. But this is completely false.

You should think highly of yourself and you should also be self-centred. Why? Because you only ever have yourself. And in a world that profits from us feeling insecure and seeking solutions to feel worthy, you should proudly express your confidence. You should take 100 selfies every day happily. If you want to be vain and stare at every mirror you walk past, then you do that. You can focus on building your physical appearance and be proud of it! It doesn't equal conceitedness, it equals inner strength.

Narcissism is characterised by a lack of empathy, sense of superiority, entitlement, exploitative habits, manipulation and a need to be admired. This goes against EVERYTHING self-love stands for. Yes, narcissists have a grandiose sense of self, but that is paired with their desire to place themselves above others due to their need for control and power. Narcissists are intentional with every decision they make because they need to create a mask which conceals their insecurity and bad intentions while chasing attention to soothe their lack of self-love and self-esteem.

Self-love is about being kinder to yourself so you can show up for your loved ones better, being so confident that you don't need to compete with anyone, knowing that you deserve to say no and rest when you need, working on your toxic traits and never needing to be admired because you are always full of self-validation. You will never catch a self-loving person criticising because they know they're not above anybody else and they're confident enough to focus on themselves without having to tear someone else down to support their own fragile ego. You can see the difference for yourself with these examples:

NARCISSISTIC THOUGHTS	SELF-LOVE THOUGHTS
'I'm perfect and flawless.'	'I'm a work in progress but I accept myself fully through my mistakes and my healing.'
'I'm always right and no one can tell me otherwise.'	'Sometimes I'm right, sometimes I'm wrong, but either way, I deserve love and kindnesses.'
'No one is good enough for me. I'm happy alone so I don't need anyone else.'	'I have high standards and boundaries to protect my precious time and energy. Companionship is of value to a good life and I deserve someone who matches my desires. I've worked on my self-love, which allows me to love others better.'
'Other people are not my problem'.	'I empathise with others, but I make sure my cup is filled first so I can serve others properly.'

Self-love vs self-care

You can do all the elaborate routines in the world but if you don't deal with the negative thought patterns that hold you back, you'll find it difficult to make any progress. Self-care is still an important part of expressing love to yourself. This practice centres around relaxation, feel-good habits and creating health and balance in our lives, which consequently has a great impact on our mental health and happiness. It trains you to value breaks and deep breaths. That you should not be a part of the moving-miles-a-minute chasing hustle culture and working-20-hours-a-day kind of life, but instead making more time for the things that really fulfil you and will sustain long-term peace.

Whereas self-love isn't all that glamorous. It's doing the hard stuff like facing your insecurities, overcoming your bad habits and working on forgiving those who have hurt you. It might mean parting ways with the temporary pleasures in your life to do better for your future self – for example, instead of eating what you want when you feel like it, you prioritise your health. Or deciding to stop spending hours reading about the latest celeb gossip and obsessing over how they look, and rather setting a limit on social media and picking up a book.

REAL self-love is on the inside. It's about accepting yourself no matter how messy your life ends up getting or how off track you go from where you thought you were supposed to be. Balancing both your self-care and self-love is the key to a healthy relationship with yourself full of boundaries, joy and confidence. Overleaf is a list of self-care and self-love practices. Try to incorporate one of each in your routine this week:

SELF-CARE HABITS	SELF-LOVE HABITS
Making time for a mani-pedi so you feel put together.	Making time to work on your self-perception until you learn that you're beautiful inside and out. This links into your inner monologue.
Going for a morning walk or to the gym.	Changing the language you use when talking about your body, removing 'good/bad body' from your vocabulary and loving it for what it is now.
Committing a day to self-maintenance by getting a haircut, doing a DIY face mask or getting a massage to inject some joy into your routine.	Taking yourself out on a date to remind yourself of the effort you deserve and to deepen the relationship you have with yourself.
Switching off in the evening with a movie, hobby or book.	Journaling before bed to reflect on what you're grateful for that day and to better understand your mind and feelings.

Self-love vs singlehood

Self-love is not a bridge between relationships, it is not simply a place for you to safely reside through break-ups, it is not reserved for when your life hits rock bottom – it is a way of living, no matter the phase of your life. Unfortunately, many assume that self-love is futile once you're in love with somebody else, but it becomes more important than ever. When you jump to pour love into others before yourself, you adopt every belief your partner has of you. You assume you deserve their silent treatment; you constantly chase their approval and, throughout this, you attach your worth more and more to another person because you didn't establish it for yourself first.

When we chase being loved, rather than loving ourselves, our partner becomes our entire universe and this is a one-way road to jealousy, possessiveness, isolation, disappointment and unfulfilled potential. You deny yourself the experience of real love when you run from dealing with yourself. Your romantic relationships mirror the relationship you have with yourself. It is why people pleasers often find themselves with narcissists – they lack boundaries, avoid conflict and chase validation, so they attract a partner who is needy, aggressive and controlling. Similarly, an insecure person will usually attract an emotionally unavailable partner because it confirms every undesirable feeling they have about their unworthiness to receive true affection, while at the same time, in their fear of being abandoned, they sabotage the relationship to avoid their partner getting too close.

Do you really have to love yourself before you can love others? Well . . . yes and no. Self-love is an ongoing journey. You need to be comfortable in your solitude before you can share your space with another to peacefully co-exist and reciprocate love healthily, but you don't need to wait until you're perfect. Romantic relationships can help us to progress on our journeys of self-love and acceptance.

So, if you have found your forever person and you're

in a happy, healthy and committed relationship, it's just as important to practise self-love as it will ensure you remain confident, independent and truly fulfilled. Every single self-love practice can be used when in a relationship. On a date with your partner in the evening? Spend the morning or afternoon alone. Celebrating Valentine's Day with your partner? Spend the day before treating and celebrating the relationship you have with yourself. Every self-love habit a single person can implement, a person in a romantic relationship can too.

These are some of the main myths surrounding self-love. I hope that you have learned that it has nothing to do with selfishness, superiority, aesthetics or 'coping mechanisms' in times of loneliness. Self-love is a necessary and continuous journey every human must go on to fulfil their full potential and achieve true self-growth.

WHY SHOULD YOU DO THIS?

'But what benefits do I really gain from putting all this work into improving my self-love?'

Great question. Self-love determines our entire lifestyle. When we truly care for ourselves, we are motivated to always act in our best interests – going after bigger opportunities, walking away from those that don't align with us, maintaining discipline to chase all of our dreams, feeding our body with a healthy diet, nourishing our soul with experiences that spark joy and believing that we are capable of everything we want. On the other hand, when we hold our insecurities and traumas, they run our reality

– we assume we are not capable of achieving, we feel judged, we settle for whatever thing or person comes our way, we overwork ourselves, we overindulge in escapism via junk food, drugs or alcohol and we accept toxic behaviour. The longer you avoid facing your self-consciousness, the worse your mental health, self-perception and life experiences will grow to be.

So, I've listed the benefits of mastering self-love in a checklist format below because once you have finished this book, you'll be able to tick each of the boxes, having experienced them all.

- ☐ I am self-assured and have mastered confidence.
- ☐ I set higher standards that result in better relationships with others.
- ☐ I am protected from toxic situations by my new boundaries.
- ☐ I overcame inner battles/turmoil to reach a sense of peace with my identity.
- ☐ I no longer chase others. Instead, I mastered detachment.
- ☐ I have a strong sense of my authentic identity which cannot be shaken by criticism from others.
- ☐ I love my reflection in the mirror. My body image and self-perception have never been better.

Now let's begin this self-love journey . . .

CHAPTER SUMMARY

- ☐ Self-love consists of taking care of your love languages, self-acceptance, self-sufficiency, self-discovery, solo dating, setting boundaries, mental health, inner monologue, inner child and confidence.
- ☐ Unlike narcissism, self-love doesn't believe in thinking you're better than others. It values confronting your flaws and accepting them as they are. It's about growing your confidence to show up for others with high capacity and security in self.
- ☐ Self-care revolves around making time for yourself to unplug, prioritise your joy and wellness and feel put together. Self-love goes deeper than the surface. It's about knowing your triggers, your wounded self, your toxic traits, where you self-sabotage, what you could improve and why you need to stop shaming and start accepting.
- ☐ Self-love is a lifelong journey. You do not need to exclude yourself from the joy and wisdom that comes from dating if you are still working through things. Self-love doesn't stop when you're in a relationship, it changes as you evolve. The important part is to always schedule time for solitude and self-reflection, so you are not floating through life blissfully unaware of the obstacles you are creating on your path because you run from dealing with your inner battles.

CHAPTER HOMEWORK

- ☐ Take the five love languages quiz online. Commit one hour this week to giving your main love language back to yourself using the examples outlined. For example, if your love language is quality time, spend your evening doing an activity you love, such as painting.
- ☐ Write out a list of the parts of you that feel harder to love unconditionally. Next to each point, question the root of this insecurity until it no longer makes sense. Start to concisely create your own definition of these features instead of accepting what society has told you to feel about it. Whether it be a large nose, acne, shyness or career expectations, begin to create a list of the qualities that actually define you – not your accomplishments or appearance, but your energy, the value you add to others' lives, your unique mindset and ideas, your compassion and empathy.
- ☐ Choose one skill you don't feel confident in and try it without asking for help. There is no need for perfection – in fact, feel free to fail, knowing it does not take away from the success of you attempting this task in the first place.
- ☐ Find some pictures or home movies of your younger self and commit some time to reliving that part of yourself. Think deeply about what you'd say to her, how you'd treat her, and now imagine that your future self currently feels that way about yourself. Let this be the start of your new, more compassionate self-dialogue.

CHAPTER 2:

'BUT I FEEL BROKEN'

How can you transform pain into power?

Is heartbreak a never-ending pain or is it a gift? A gift leading you to a lesson that is likely to change your life for the better? I am a firm believer that pain is never personal. The universe handpicks adversities for us throughout our lives to unlock the inner strength we already possess so that we can overcome them. When you shift your perspective, break-ups become a doorway to endless possibility and opportunity just waiting to be uncovered. We have all encountered at least one person who has suffered through a bitter break-up only to come out of the other side more radiant, successful and joyful. So often, you can feel their relief in knowing they *will* love again and they *will* love better. After all, other people are experiences, not the determinants of ourselves and our futures. However, while all of that is true, we must acknowledge the difficulty of picking up the broken pieces of our heart and choosing to move on when the pain is still fresh, and this is how . . .

PROCESSING THE LOSS

Leaving someone

When you decide to break things off, a lot of guilt can come with that. Especially if you are familiar with the feeling of heartache, making you reluctant to inflict that pain on another human being. Walking away from a situation that didn't feel right for you is a huge accomplishment: you honoured your intuition and withdrew your love when you were no longer comfortable sharing it with that person. That is commendable. It is courageous to speak up when the love is no longer serving you, instead of anxiously stringing someone's heart along in the hope that everything will 'just be okay'. A relationship does not need to go terribly wrong for you to justify ending it. The dates could be extravagantly planned and your partner could be the most romantic you've ever experienced, yet you can still decide it's not right for you.

Too many people stay because of the fear of having to start all over getting to know new people, or just waiting for their partner to live up to the image they created of them in their head. But instead, you should stay because it's a love that makes you wake up every day in awe of the gift that is getting to share your life with them. You deserve the kind of love you always dreamed of and when you walk away from the relationships that fall short of your ideal, you finally take control of your future.

Our biggest downfall is doubt. Many couples that stay together for too long do so purely out of fear that the grass won't be greener on the other side, but, guess what . . . it always is. Your loss of connection is a sign that it is time to move on.

It is a symbol of your growth and that there will be another relationship that aligns better with the person you are evolving into. There will never be doubt when you realise that you will always attract the energy that you desire and mirror. What is there really to doubt then? You would never find yourself wanting to walk away from something if it was really meant for you. You went after something you once craved, tried it on for size and decided it wasn't the right fit – that's just what dating is. Some people will try to shame you for leaving when 'you had it good' but, truthfully, many of them can't comprehend the process of choosing yourself. No matter why you decide to leave – to focus on yourself, find a better partner or escape a lifestyle you never signed up for – you are honouring your needs and that is something to be proud of.

Battling heartbreak

To lose the person you talked to every single day, who was always there, who knew all your secrets and who you adored more than anything is to experience the kind of grief that should not be rushed. Feel your feelings, spend the day in bed, cry it all out, vent to your girlfriends, scribble an angry journal entry, watch a sad film, lose yourself to an Adele album and finish the pint of ice cream, so you can be done with it.

The more you rush the healing process and push the difficult emotions away, the longer it will take to recover. It is easy to lose yourself in the pain when you obsess over the thought of them without you, and while it is normal to grieve, allowing your emotions to assume answers to situations you have no knowledge of is never the solution. Instead, it is your responsibility to reconnect to the person you once were. How did you spend your time before they dominated it? What brought you joy before you had any dates planned? Where was your happy place before you found yourself in their arms? It's up to you to create new experiences of happiness so you don't falsely attach the feeling to a person you no longer have access to.

I made the mistake of revolving my daily routine around my ex for months after our break-up; he was the centre of my every decision when he didn't even think about me anymore. I'd only listen to love songs that reminded me of his presence, I only dated men to replicate the way he used to make me feel and I spent every evening revisiting our life together through places and pictures. I was trapped living in the past for eight months because it felt comfortable. But comfort is a one-way street to staying in the same place your entire life. When you allow the desire for ease to guide you, you will always be led astray.

Break-ups are supposed to feel like hell. The process of breaking an attachment you wanted to last forever will tear you apart, but it will also teach you life-changing lessons. Embracing the hardship allows you to see the opportunity in loss, while running away from it keeps you wrapped up in daydreams of delusion. The best way to come around from heartbreak is logic, something often lacking at this stage.

Really think about it:

- Did they actually deserve you?
- Did they treat you how you always envisioned your dream partner would?

- Was it real love? Full of reciprocated affection, respect, commitment, trust, communication, care and recognition?
- Are they the only person on this planet who is capable of making you love so greatly?
- Who told you this was as good as it was going to get for you?
- Was it really right person, wrong time or just wrong person, right lesson?

The aftermath of toxic love

When you've escaped the situation but the intensity of the hurt remains every single day, a complicated feeling of never-ending addiction that isolates you from all other areas of your life, this may be the sign of a toxic lover. This addiction stems from the abuser's favourite tool – trauma bonding. This is characterised by a rollercoaster relationship interchanging the highest of highs and the most hurtful of lows to the point you wake up every day wondering if you'll fall asleep crying or beaming with affection. Longing for the return of your toxic partner is understandable in this situation despite what your friends might exclaim.

In these sorts of relationships, you are sold a dream and faced with a nightmare. You don't leave because trauma bonds function and holds the same power as drug addiction. You become invested and hopeful with every grandiose gesture and loving word which has you confusing their mistreatment of you as love. Almost every day, you justify their bad behaviour because they have carefully integrated moments of satisfaction and affirmation throughout. The gradual manipulation process tricks you into forgiving their destruction because it is followed by positive reinforcement. One second, they're screaming at you and the next they're cradling you, professing their undying loyalty and love for you. Therefore, every time you attempt to withdraw, you feel overwhelmed because you are practically rewarded each time you endure the pain they inflict. This forces you into a never-ending cycle of ups and downs, always chasing the dopamine hit. Dopamine is often referred to as 'the happy hormone' due to its integral role in our brain's reward system. Anytime you experience pleasure, your dopamine levels spike – this instant 'high' can become addictive. Our brain comes to associate abuse with love and we become oblivious to the suffering we endure.

Our childhood (something completely out of our control) can lead us to walk down paths blind to red flags like love bombing or even aggression because we seek out the familiarity of what we grew up with and then label it as love. If you grew up with chaos, tough love, a complete lack of affection or deep insecurity, you are not to be blamed for confusing your abuser for your soulmate. So you must not feel shameful in this situation. Expecting ourselves to consistently make the correct decision completely deprives us of self-compassion – a key element of self-love. Instead, it's your duty to alter what you see as familiar. The only way to achieve this and remove all possibility of giving our hearts to destructive love once again is through building the strongest relationship to self.

Before you concern yourself with how you wish to be treated

in future romantic relationships, you must be obsessed with how you treat yourself and what you allow yourself to tolerate. This can start small, like being gentle with yourself and speaking kinder words when you fail, and then grow larger, to evaluating the friendships and the company you have around you. You are worthy of people whose presence leaves you feeling energised and positively influenced.

Friendship endings

To outgrow a friend is normal and a necessary part of life. It is actually a milestone to be celebrated because it represents the evolution you need to fulfil your potential and reach the kind of life you dream about. Your aspirations are only possible via change, otherwise you would already have achieved them. While hard work and learning are vital within this process, the relationships you tolerate play a much larger role. The people we surround ourselves with affect our values, interests, priorities, routines, confidence, mindset, self-perception and beliefs. When we are on the road to growing into the next version of ourselves, we must leave behind certain ideas and habits to get there. With this comes the people who refuse to progress, while holding onto the idea of a previous version of you that you are trying to release. During this process, many of us make the mistake of remaining attached to what we're used to (the friends who have been by our side thus far) at the expense of what we could be (the highest version of ourselves who achieves everything we once thought was unreachable). The only attachment you should ever have is the one to yourself and it is your duty to put your future first because it is the only thing you can control.

Friendships, however longstanding, do not define your life, *you do* that. You get to wake up and make entirely different choices, you get to surround yourself with different minds that align with the new path you may be embarking on, you get to reinvent yourself, think differently, act differently. See how this loss can actually be an opportunity? But I'll get into this in the next section.

Having said that, of course you should hold on to the memories and cherish them forever, because aside from the ending, our ex-friends got us through a lot of pivotal moments and the good moments always outweigh the bad. They were a safe place and a shoulder to lean on at one point, so we should remain grateful for that love, while remembering we will experience it again. Other people are just as complex as we are, with entire histories we know nothing about, tiny details that craft significant parts of their decisions, unique aspirations, complicated self-perceptions and daily inner battles we couldn't even begin to imagine. Nothing is ever personal. People act based on their unique journey, not yours – an argument, lack of closure or loss in connection is fate's way of separating your previously intertwined paths because they are no longer going in parallel.

Specific people come into our lives at different points to help us face our obstacles, progress on our journey, or learn more about ourselves or what we want in life. When their purpose is fulfilled, the alignment breaks and we come across the next friendship that teaches us the next necessary lesson, helping us to grow into who we were always meant to be. You will meet more like-minded individuals who align with who you've grown to be, who will inspire you and lead you to the next phase. Remember that you are the main character, your life is like a movie and if things stayed the same with zero plot twists – well . . . who would want to watch that? *Yawn*.

Losing yourself

To no longer recognise yourself is the start of the journey to finding yourself. We grow up accepting what we've been given. The friends we made because of proximity, the job we took for convenience, the lifestyle we lived because of our parents, the love we accepted as we didn't know any better. We lose ourselves in this chaos because we're chasing what we're *supposed* to want and who we're *supposed* to be so that we can please everyone around us.

How can we ever truly know ourselves when we're constantly performing for others and just trying to stay afloat every day in the fast-moving current of life? People waste years going through the motions instead of consciously crafting their life and their self-concept. I am no exception. I was stuck on a loop of trying to get through the day with all of the commotion running wild through my head: 'Study harder', 'Don't let your family down', 'Why don't you have a boyfriend yet?' 'It's weird that you only have three friends, make more', 'But what will they think?', 'That's cringey', 'Why can't you just be normal?', 'I can't believe you made such a stupid mistake – don't you feel embarrassed?', 'They don't even like you', 'You don't make enough money', 'Your life is so boring', 'You're probably just going to mess it all up again'.

We mistakenly accept others' definition of who we are. When your family reminds you that you're not living up to their expectations for you, it translates to low confidence in every other area of your life. When you become a target for judgement and backhanded compliments at school, your once normal reflection in the mirror starts getting more and more distorted every day. When meeting new people results in being spoken over and forgotten about, you label yourself socially awkward and undesirable. Consequently, you wake up every day living as a watered down variation of yourself to make yourself more digestible and likeable to others because of the perceptions you've internalised for years. The truth is that no one will ever have a valid opinion of you and every single person on this planet is incapable of understanding you. Your parents, siblings, best friends, peers and strangers on the street have all constructed completely different versions of 'you' in each of their minds based on their own life experiences, traumas, preferences, life lessons, life view, values and self-perception.

How beautiful and freeing is that? There's so much liberation in realising the only person who will ever have a valid opinion of you is *you*. You are the only person who has experienced every passing thought in your mind, has been by your side every single second from the moment you were born, understands every emotion you tried to push away and is aware of every experience you've lived in every area of your life – no one else comes close to knowing your life in that way.

REFRAMING YOUR MINDSET

~~Unfortunately~~ We've all experienced some kind of trauma and heartache. I wanted to strike through 'unfortunately' because only the strongest individuals receive the gift of adversity. Embrace your suffering, it contains all the necessary lessons you need to get closer to the one person who will always be there for you – you. Ninety-nine per cent of the population falls into the trap of collecting their miseries to complain about how others are so privileged in comparison. This act of self-harm can take shape in a number of forms:

1. Concerning yourself with how others live

You will be unable to make any progress if you focus only on what you lack. When you obsess over people and things out of your control, you abandon all things 'self' – love, growth, care and confidence. Do you really want to spend energy on building up your sense of hopelessness through living vicariously on how amazing people's lives look from afar – which never quite matches up to how it looks and feels when you're really in it?

2. Assuming 'other people have it better than you'

Our opinion and perceptions are a result of the narratives we have created in our minds. We can convince ourselves that others are in better positions in life when in actuality, we don't know the full story of their reality or the struggle that got them there. When you focus on stalking carefully curated social media highlights, fixating on how well someone was dressed one day or assuming the few stories they chose to tell you represent what their entire life looks like, then of course they will always be winning in comparison. This is a form of self-sabotage which stems from deep insecurity in our own lives. You are putting your confidence into other people rather than yourself.

3. Lowering your energetic vibration

Your vibrational frequency is the intensity and quality of energy that you are operating with and experiencing. Dr Shawna Freshwater PhD explains, 'Emotions resonate with the vibrational frequency that they generate. The higher the vibrational frequency, then the higher the expansion, and the greater the Life Force in your cells.' High vibrational people have mastered the art of living at a higher energy frequency. These are enlightenment (700+), peace (600), love (500) and acceptance (350), measured in the hertz frequency. As a result, they feel more gratitude and joy. Our vibrational energy is something we can change consciously through the actions we carry out every day. When you complain and compare, you are living in the lowest energetic frequencies: anger (150), desire (125), grief (75), guilt (30) and, the lowest of all, shame (20).

Every time you choose self-doubt over self-belief, judgement over acceptance and shame over compassion, you lower your vibration, which affects the life you live. This is because our thoughts and feelings (which create our vibrational frequency) influence the perception we have of our circumstances and therefore the opportunities we grasp – or in this case – miss out on. This scale of emotional frequencies was originally coined by Dr David Hawkins in his book, *The Map of Consciousness Explained: A Proven Energy Scale to Actualize Your Ultimate Potential*, to track our levels of consciousness based on the vibrations we produce from the emotions we feel.

THE EMOTIONAL VIBRATION FREQUENCY CHART

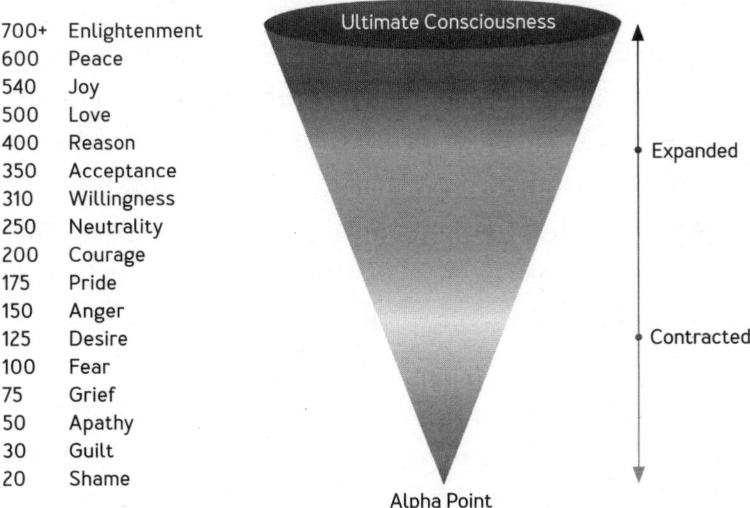

4. Being oblivious of your own blessings

This external focus will not affect the other person, but it will make you blind to the piles of privilege you currently possess that dozens of people wish they had as they compare themselves to you. While others have it so much easier because they started off in life on a higher rung on the ladder, crowds of people on rungs beneath you hope to have had the chances you did. To truly give ourselves the best shot at a life well lived we must acknowledge the beauty in the life we are currently living in order to progress onto the next improved version of it. Otherwise, we will be at the mercy of people we hardly know anything about for the rest of our lives.

5. Rejecting the lessons you could be taking advantage of

Every time you engage in victim mentality you parade your lack of self-belief, which signals to yourself and everyone else that you are not capable of actualising your desires. If you make the conscious decision to feel pity for the bad days you inevitably survived, you will still stay cemented in the past rather than using the treasure box of wisdom that comes with every heartache to your advantage. Adversity is never personal. It is life's way of sending you down a path of *temporary* failure so that you can learn more about yourself, or the world, or your job, or other people to help you grow as a person, which then gets you further in making those desires into achievements.

6. Surrendering your power

You don't want to be waiting for something outside of yourself to come and save you. Waiting for the right time, a different person, a better job, a promotion, an improved appearance or the correct amount of knowledge before you start is self-sabotage. You must take responsibility for your life immediately if you are dissatisfied with it. You were given your unique path because you are strong enough to live it. *You* are the one who has crafted who you are today by getting through every moment thus far. No one else could possibly have the tools and knowledge to break you out of your own life than you do, because their paths are nothing like yours, and that is your superpower.

Adversity is a gift

What is life without the bad moments? A mundane existence of predictability and consistent emotion that robs us of the privilege of experiencing the full spectrum of human emotion. When we fail to see the hope in hardship, we sacrifice our ability to change adversity into accomplishment.

This was a very long-winded journey for me. I grew up with a very unordinary childhood compared to my friends. My dad left when I was two years old. To this day, I have no memory or knowledge of him, and I don't know anything about that entire side of my bloodline. It was never something that concerned me, though, because my stepdad soon came into the picture and effortlessly became my first best friend.

We were the perfect little suburban family until my parents moved three hours away from me when I was seven years old, leaving me to live with my grandparents. They divorced two years later and I was left with no relationship with or sight of my stepdad ever again – not even a goodbye. It broke me. There wasn't much conversation about this in my family; it was swept under the rug and they assumed that my 11-year-old self would just be okay . . . and I resented the world for it. I carried these suppressed emotions for the next decade. I would feel my heart drop when I sat among the wholesome normality of a Tuesday evening in my best friend's house, eating dinner and watching a movie with her parents. I wondered why such a simple and loving experience was taken from me at such a young age. I never told anybody about it, of course. The indifferent nature of my other family members taught me otherwise: it's not a big deal. Don't be so emotional. This is *your* normal. Accept it. This created a breeding ground for my inner pity party.

I always felt so unlucky in life until I started to focus on my future instead of my past. See, every day, my wounded mindset would allow me to find some element of pain I had experienced in the past in my present moment, which prolonged my suffering and made me feel like my pain was never-ending. I wasn't giving myself the chance to experience a better life, where I didn't think about what I had lost but instead everything that I could gain. So, eventually, I told myself I had to make the adversity worth it; I couldn't just let it remain there to haunt me, but instead I needed to use it as a motivator to create the life of my dreams.

I used my pain to create my happiness by changing my perspective of triggering events. When I saw a little girl walking in the street holding hands with her parents, I started looking in admiration of the abundance of love that exists in the world. I also changed myself. For so long, I fetishised my sadness and made my traumas my identity. Instead, I shifted my identity to the luckiest girl alive. Quite a jump I know, but it worked. I realised the past doesn't exist; it is simply an accumulation of memories in my mind that receives whatever level of attention that I decide. So I adjusted that focus to 'future memories', which is the process of imagining your future before it has even happened. This is when I really started manifesting before I was even fully aware of the concept. Daydreaming about a reality where you get everything you want is such a powerful manifestation tool because your brain cannot tell the difference between a real or imagined experience, so it starts building the necessary neural pathways and thought patterns needed to attract that lifestyle.

Suddenly, my confidence and self-belief improved. I was no longer defining my life by the events so far but rather all the possibilities to come and the way I decided to feel *today*. I stopped keeping count of all the bad things that have happened, as if life was using me as its own personal dartboard, and I recognise how every misery has made me into the person I am today. I saw that without having to somehow figure out the way around new obstacles, I would hardly have the knowledge that pushes me through the doors that have made my life so much bigger today. I am not my past; I am how I choose to see and live in the moment I am experiencing right now. I stopped expecting instant results and using each failed attempt to define whether I was capable. It's okay to fall down a few hundred times in a row because there's always the chance that I win the 386th time I try. And even if I don't, it's still all part of the journey of trying new things, removing the things that don't serve me, learning more about what I want and building a better foundation to conquer the next pursuit that truly matters.

Of course, bad things still happened – bullying, heartbreak, betrayal, depression, loneliness to name a few. Equally, as I sit here writing this book from the apartment I once dreamed of living in, I am fully aware of all the obstacles to come and I welcome them, because they won't break me, they'll make me 10 times stronger. There has never been an adversity that I didn't bounce back from as a 2.0 version of myself, regardless of the time it took to get there.

Nowadays, I no longer look at hardships as a personal

problem but rather a gift from the universe that allows me to learn the necessary resilience and lessons needed at this stage so I can progress onto the next level. You can't just dream about where you want to be, you have to be the kind of person who's ready for that lifestyle and every challenge that comes with it. Embracing your obstacles is the only way to get there.

Stepping into your power

Let's dissect this further. A break-up is your opportunity to find yourself again after the experience of being in a partnership. You won't be the same person, so don't feel disheartened by the confusion of feeling distant from your previous single self but instead awakened by the prospect of who you get to become with the life experience you've just gained.

Welcome to the ultimate storyline of your new villain era. No, not the one that makes you mistrustful, malicious and cold in deliberate isolation. The villain arc that forces you to step into your power – better boundaries, new makeover, fiercer energy, contagious aura, stronger self-worth, focusing on yourself 24/7. Experiencing attachment just to get your heart broken and only having yourself to pick up the pieces is how you learn how to master detachment.

Detachment is the process of letting go from outcomes. This concept comes from Morrie Schwartz's theory, which discusses the importance of presence and separating one's emotions, by feeling and processing each feeling before choosing to move on from them. The aim is to no longer feel the need to control people, force situations or wish people into your future before they have earned their place there. The laws of detachment prioritise maintaining emotional balance. This is achieved through the awareness that uncertainty and loss is a given, fear of success and failure is pointless, and, most importantly, people are never ours, they are merely experiences given to us for the timelines we need them – not want them. When you finally release expectations of others and instead only focus on what you can control (yourself), your life will no longer be constrained by another person's actions.

It doesn't matter how it ends because you were always fully present in enjoying their presence in the moment with acceptance that it might not last forever and that's okay, it doesn't make the relationship any less significant. People come into our lives for a day, month or decade to serve their purpose in crafting who we are meant to be. Once you realise this, you will grieve and you will reminisce, but you will never have to chase, beg, prove your worth or settle below what you deserve *ever* again. This fearlessness translates to stronger confidence in setting your boundaries without fear of upsetting the other person because you know you'll always have yourself.

When someone plays with your heart and leaves you doubting if you're good enough you have lost yourself, but you are also presented with a blank canvas on which to recreate yourself. The relationship you have with yourself is your most powerful resource, even if we are hardly given any time to build it among all our other daily stresses and to-do lists. There is no greater motivator and isolator than heartache. You must make change your new number one priority. Trying new hobbies, visiting new places and talking to new people will grant you the biggest leaps in self-transformation, leaving you cringing at what you tolerated in your old life.

Aside from redefining your comfort zones, you must redefine your self-concept. We go through life struggling with insecurities, insults and ill-treatment from others because of the meaning we associate with these things. We are so used to internalising everyone else's beliefs of us because we haven't taken the time to consciously decide who we are. But the truth is, *you* put meaning to words and situations, not the other way around.

When you have affirmed the abundance of beauty you already possess without waiting for anyone else to validate it, criticisms and insults become so hard to believe, they might as well be claiming you have blue-coloured skin. You find every negative comment to be that bizarre because you have an unbreakable definition of every aspect of your identity.

You form improved beliefs on your self-concept through every action you take. Every decision you make helps form the type of person you become. For example, when you text your friends asking if your selfie is Instagram-worthy, you are identifying as the type of person who needs external validation to feel comfortable with themselves. In comparison, when you wear the outfit you like without worrying how dressy it is and then step out in public to dine alone and make friendly conversation with your server, you identify as the type of person who is sure of themselves, self-validating and prioritises themselves before pleasing others.

Our biggest mistake is using our current limiting beliefs to make our decisions for us, as this keeps us in the same self-loathing place for our entire lives. Instead, if your limiting belief is that you're too shy to post on social media, but you carry out the habit of your desired self-concept – in this case to post as if it's a skill that comes to you naturally – you embody the traits that would empower you until they naturally become a part of who you are. You can't help but fall completely in love with yourself once you've developed the self-respect to always do what you first intended and live for the benefit of who you are growing into instead of in fear of what the past used to tell you. Eventually, you become unrecognisable, and the people who once had you self-doubting are long forgotten.

CHAPTER SUMMARY

- [ ] Heartache helps grow our strength and resilience. These skills stay with us and allow our relationships in all areas of life to get better as we continue to evolve and learn more about what we will and will not tolerate. It is a blessing that gives us quality time to set out our standards and critically question what aligns to us, rather than chasing after fickle qualities and advice that matches other people's needs but leaves us unfulfilled.
- [ ] Outgrowing people and ending friendships that once were the centre of our universe are a normal and necessary part of life. It is a beautiful sign of our evolution and alignment to our true path. We risk stagnating when we place attachment to others over completing the potential of who we could be and the new places and people we could experience. Allow yourself to enjoy the present without placing people in your future before they've earned their place there.
- [ ] Losing yourself is a result of living according to the definitions other people place on you. How can you know yourself when you've never made the time to decide who you want to be? Every single person in our lives experiences us in a completely different light based on their own life experience, lessons, mindset and traumas – therefore, only you will ever have a valid opinion of yourself.
- [ ] Stepping into your power is the result of embracing the bad moments and using them to your advantage.

They are all lessons that will make you into a stronger and smarter version of yourself every single time. Trying something new with the arrival of each new obstacle or adversity is how you speed up your self-transformation and become unrecognisable.

CHAPTER HOMEWORK

- ☐ Write a list of every ex-partner or former friend you've had and bullet point what you learned from the breakdown of that bond. You'll be surprised at the lessons that came about from those experiences and how you've changed as a result of that new wisdom. It will change the narrative from failures to necessary enlightenments. You might also discover connecting qualities between these relationships and realise patterns that may have led you to go after the same type of person, which in turn will allow you clarity in who you pursue next time.
- ☐ Missing someone you know you shouldn't be with? Write a list of all the reasons they're not meant for you. Nostalgia is masterful in hiding away the truth and blinding you with only fond memories which clouds your judgement. Come back to this list every time you feel yourself romanticising a bond that's not meant for you. Now create an outline of your dream partner. What standards will you not compromise on anymore? What do you deserve? How do you wish to be treated? Allow this to be a reminder that better possibilities are out there and you sacrifice these every time you run back to the past.

- [ ] Start planning the future of your dreams to prevent your sadness of the past killing your vibration and keeping you in a reality which no longer exists. Create a vision board to help you visualise where you could be to disassociate yourself from moments that no longer exist. Pairing this with a daily or weekly gratitude journaling session is a great way to take control of your mood and create happiness now instead of waiting for the right situation to create it for you.

CHAPTER 3:

FALLING OFF THE SELF-LOVE WAGON

Why is loving yourself so difficult?

GROWING PAINS

Meeting new versions of yourself can often result in a craving to mourn who you used to be and feeling like you're losing previous ideals of your life and what it could've been. We are constantly evolving – our bodies alter, our favourite people leave, our careers can be taken, our living situation can change in a second, our decision making can be unexpected and suddenly we find ourselves hard to recognise – but that's the beauty of it. To acknowledge that beauty we must remove attachment from the ideals we have of ourselves and only then can we flourish. We place so much expectation on ourselves because we attach our worth and self-love to labels like academics, career, wealth, popularity, looks and status instead of who we are at our core. You are not your body nor your appearance, they are simply a vessel that holds your true value – your soul, your heart, your thoughts and your energy.

One day, I was a final-year university student sitting in my bedroom and smiling at the realisation that my appearance is the least interesting thing about me. It holds so little importance because I offer so much more value as a person! There is so much to love and understand about me! I think deeply, I'm funny, creative, thoughtful, hopelessly romantic, compassionate and a big dreamer . . . those are only the qualities off the top of my head. There is so much beauty in my personality, in how I view the world and how I approach obstacles. There's even more mystery in the beauty others see in me – I have no idea as to how I've impacted everyone I've come across in my lifetime. Whether they still smile at our memories, giggle at an old joke I told, find comfort in a pep talk I once offered or simply used my temporary presence as a crucial lesson to help them move to the next phase of their life, my *presence* matters more than my crooked nose and tummy bloat.

This realisation completely shifted how I carried myself. The next day, I got a fringe cut in my hair, got my nose pierced and started wearing grunge fashion. I knew the haircut didn't suit my face shape, but it was temporary. I knew the nose ring was risky, but I could always take it out. And I knew the clothing wasn't flattering but it was fun to experiment! I started seeing my body merely as my own personal avatar to customise whenever I wish, instead of continuing the torturous cycle of amending my looks according to trends, what men would be attracted to and what would make me more worthy of compliments. This allowed me to detach from the previous expectations

I had held about myself because I was no longer validating them through living my life to meet them.

You are not *where* you are in life but rather *who* you become in those places. You left your job, lost some money or failed a test? Okay, lesson learned! But it doesn't define you. In my first year of university, I felt so deeply ashamed of myself that I could barely recognise myself. I felt like I became the most irresponsible, naïve version of myself overnight. So, I had to get uncomfortable and face the things I disliked most about myself:

1. I was losing my sense of self to chase male validation.
2. I was abandoning my academic potential out of FOMO.
3. My days revolved around chasing dopamine and comfort rather than working on my goals.
4. I made decisions to control others' perception of me rather than developing the view I had of myself.

It felt disappointing to admit but once I did, I had one of two options: use these things to facilitate my self-loathing *or* use them to my advantage to build my self-love. I went with the latter.

This process began with forgiving myself. Once I began to understand how I was led into each of those situations, I could understand myself and my triggers more. For example, I chased male validation because I had always been in a relationship, I had never worked on my insecurities and this was a quick fix to raise my self-esteem, which I knew would give me that dopamine distraction. This understanding gave me more self-compassion so I could step away from shaming myself to forgiving my mistakes.

I also realised it was harder to detach from men's opinions when I was out partying and dating. My triggers were my social life (the environments I was placing myself in) and the importance I placed on my appearance, which inevitably made me lose a lot of myself to vanity and shallowness. From there, I started saying no to party invites and instead staying at home to work on my creative passions. I also stopped dating and replaced it with quality time spent developing my bond with friends or meeting new people. When I needed something fun to do, I would go on a solo date to museums, bookstores, restaurants or simply to explore cities alone. This then fostered an environment in which I could learn more about myself, free from external perceptions.

I analysed each of the four items on the list of things I disliked about myself in the same way before acting to transform those lessons into ones of self-love. But ultimately, it was about self-compassion and realising that making mistakes is indispensable in self-growth. Shaming yourself for messing up or not staying on track is teaching yourself that you must get it right 100 per cent of the time – but this is your first time going through life, so why place such harsh expectations on yourself?

Others might try to shame you for your mistakes, but you did all you could with the knowledge and resources gathered on your personal life path so far. Beating yourself up for your mistakes makes you fearful of failing next time when you should be embracing those moments. So have faith in failing, knowing that you will provide yourself with the wisdom needed to commence the next level of your life. And you will be able to do this twice as fast when you are not always waiting to make the correct step, attempting to swerve any risk.

Although I was once a 19-year-old filled with guilt, I am now 23, looking back on those same mistakes in gratitude because they all influenced me to become better. I feel lucky to have failed and fallen so frequently before most have even started. Mistake-making is life's way of teaching you how to fall in love with yourself. You can't love someone you don't know, but the more you learn about them and every aspect of their personality, the more life you experience together and the more challenges you jointly overcome, then the more you will discover about them that there is to love – and the same goes for yourself.

What if you feel you're not as happy as you thought you would be? When we're younger, we imagine how magical and abundant our lives will be in our teens or our twenties, but then we may find ourselves dragging our feet miserably through those years instead, wondering what went wrong. I've found the cause of this disappointment is attachment to your expectations. I grew up imagining every part of my life before I even stepped into it. I was horrified when I found myself finishing university without the strong female friendship group I thought I'd have. I felt defeated at 22, living at home, barely making a liveable salary, getting rejected from jobs and watching my peers succeed on social media. I constantly questioned whether my social life was good enough, if my relationship was right, if I could be doing more. As soon as I let go of the expectation of where I should be, there was nothing left to criticise myself for. I needed to lessen the influence of my past. Versions of myself that hadn't experienced this much life yet, versions that were too idealistic, versions that had no idea what was to come.

The truth is, in this present moment you are more equipped to handle the life you've been given because you have lived more of it. Why would you feel bad for not living up to standards that were created by a version of you that hadn't even experienced this phase of your life? How were they supposed to know what would be best for you right this moment? How would they ever know what battles you were about to fight that caused you to get to this moment? Only present you can understand why you're here and make the conscious decision to realise you are always where you were meant to be.

Even through the struggle and pain, these are necessary moments in your life which provide you with resilience, empathy and growth, better equipping you to deal with the life to come – if you were always wondering where you should be, you would never grow because you're ignoring all of the lessons handed to you right now, and if you never grow, you stay the exact same person in the exact same place your entire life. You are always *meant* for love and joy but that can only be achieved through taking the wisdom needed in our adversity so that we can evolve into the people who know how to create and receive all the abundance we deserve.

Looking back, I wasn't supposed to have the friendship circle I dreamed of in university and my failure to obtain it allowed me to hone in on my creativity and embrace solitude. I had so much time to develop my relationship with myself and to make major strides in progressing in my aspirations. Eventually, I had all the freedom I needed to move to another city, live alone and start over. As a result, I met people who were more aligned, helped me on my growth journey and influenced my business for the better – all of which inevitably made me more successful.

Sometimes the things we think we want are rooted in familiarity and comparison, when really we are meant for much bigger things and our lives will present us with hurdle after hurdle until we understand that we need to change things or try a different path. I'm so thankful I didn't end up with my first crush, became a part of those friendship groups or went after the career that made sense at that point in my life. Paying more attention to how my life events were unfolding helped me to discover my true potential that my past self was so unaware of. That unawareness had me planning out my life according to the friendships I already had, the relationships I had already been in, the career paths I had been taught about – how could I maximise my potential if I was always basing my decisions on a past life that clearly didn't get me what I wanted? So, the next time things feel unexpected or you're trying something new without instant success, remember that you're living in a way your future self will thank you for . . . and that means letting go of your past self, for now.

Sometimes, we hold ourselves back from our growth journey because of the people we surround ourselves with. These people aren't necessarily bad, but they've been in your life for a long time and naturally they've formed a certain perception of you and placed you in a neat box in their mind to categorise you, alongside all the other people in their life. The second you decide to grow and change and experiment, you step out of that box and therefore risk looking 'cringey' to the people who have always known you because you are going against their expectations and what is familiar about you. It's normal to doubt whether you should take a step in doing something out of character, but part of self-love is acknowledging this feeling and doing it anyway, and not allowing how other people define you to control your actions.

There can be a small element of people pleasing here – we waited so long to get friends like these or worked so hard to be accepted by our family members and now we risk upsetting the balance in our relationships. When you are afraid of living differently or standing out, you put the power in other people's hands. But when you operate from a place of self-love, you focus on your own opinions first. You make it a habit to ask yourself what would make you happy, how this would align to your future. When you practise this thought process, you eventually condition yourself to filter out the voices of everybody else, who can either try to get on board or reveal themselves as inauthentic supporters of you. This is also why I think break-ups should be celebrated. When you stay within the limits of the people you've known your whole life, you are bound to stay the person you were when you met them, but when you enter new rooms with new people, you are encouraged to rediscover and find the new you.

In the end, loving yourself is only difficult when you're more focused on the outer world over your inner world. Your status, success, appearance, lifestyle and relationships do not define you. We feel unlovable because of rejection, the internalisation of others' opinions, how we are treated and our experiences with love, but all these things are out of our control; they simply happen to us and are often representative of someone else's beliefs or demons that are projected onto us. So how could they accurately reflect who we are and thus how lovable we are? Instead, what really defines you is your perspective. Loving yourself feels natural when every past mistake is seen as an opportunity for self-compassion, when every limiting belief can create better self-understanding and when every day, no matter how good or bad, is a chance for gratitude and acceptance to be in this particular body, on this life path with so much freedom to change and grow at any moment in time.

HOW SOCIETY TEACHES US TO HATE OURSELVES

Society, media and businesses make money from generating new insecurities and ideals that you should follow to be 'normal' and desirable. 'Your skin is too textured', 'Your lips aren't plump enough', 'Your nails are the wrong shape', 'Your hips should be rounder', 'Your job isn't impressive', 'Your weekends look boring', 'Your wardrobe isn't trendy anymore' – constant messages that make us feel like there's something wrong with us and how we live our lives.

It's profitable to always have you chasing the next best thing and never quite feeling good enough – especially when you're trapped in the online loop of self-comparison. Self-comparison stems from psychologist Leon Festinger's social comparison theory, which states that people determine their own worth and value by comparing how they stack up against others. The constant exposure to every possible lifestyle and possibility, refreshed at your fingertips every 0.1 seconds, keeps you controllable. There are always more things to buy, new ways to 'look better' and 'get fitter'. Millions of solutions to be just about anybody but yourself.

What they don't tell you is none of these beauty standards are true. There are about 8 billion people on this planet who hold different ideas of beauty. One person could say there's nothing too striking about your face and another might say you have the most unique features they've ever seen. There's no point in waiting for someone to vouch for your desirability because no matter how perfect you look, there will always be a crowd of people ready to tell you otherwise. And that's okay because opinions can't tell your truth . . . you get to decide that.

From the age of 11, I was bullied for my nose that took up too much space on my small face. The boy I liked ridiculed me for it and I remembered his comment every time I looked in a mirror for the next decade. When I was 15, I finally worked up the courage to ask my family for a nose job and to my surprise they agreed, on the condition I waited until I was 18. So I happily waited for the day I would finally feel beautiful.

A few years later, I was starting university and in the process of reinventing myself. I had spent my school years hiding myself away because of my insecurities, so I decided to walk into this new phase of my life with an alter ego – a character that would embody everything I lacked, from confidence to social skills and breathtaking beauty. Nothing actually changed apart from the fact I got some contact lenses, learned how to apply makeup and acted like I wasn't absolutely petrified when walking up to strangers and starting conversations.

Three years flew by and all of a sudden I was 21 years old and finishing my degree. The entire time, I hadn't thought about the nose job I'd wished for so badly in my early teens because I realised my life was perfectly fine without it.

I successfully made friends with new people, I dated the guys I liked, I stopped hiding my face in photos, I had the courage to start posting videos online and . . . I liked myself throughout it all. At university, there was always something to do, some place to go or some new person to talk to and that experience alone built up my confidence. This was when I realised my appearance was actually the least interesting thing about me. Now, I occasionally see a photograph of myself taken in unflattering lighting that makes my nose appear 10 times bigger, but I post the photo anyway.

How did I get here? By choosing what my perception of beauty is. I have given myself the permission to accept my appearance for what it is. I know my body and face still look the same and no amount of extra photos taken will make me 'look better'. I don't berate my looks after seeing myself in a group photo because when someone talks about beauty, I imagine *myself*, not perfectly retouched models I've seen in magazines. It's a conscious decision. For example, small lips are only seen as 'unattractive' because of the meaning you assign to them. It's a result of the narrative you have accepted from the choices that other people make and the new standards of beauty that the cosmetic industry is trying to feed you.

Celebrities from Zendaya to Priyanka Chopra have spoken out about their experiences in image altering and having their bodies photoshopped to the point where they didn't even recognise themselves. Let me remind you that some of the most alluring women recognised worldwide – Jennifer Aniston, Reese Witherspoon, Emma Watson, Cara Delevingne, Catherine, Princess of Wales and Nina Dobrev to name but a few – all have naturally thin lips they choose to embrace because *they* are the deciders of their beauty, and the world often follows along if you carry those beliefs with confidence.

As for keeping up with the Joneses and trying to appear as successful as possible, I fell flat on my face into this trap. I used my envy as ambition, and I thought it was the healthiest decision I could make. Every designer bag and lavish home I saw on social media convinced me I wasn't working hard enough. Every morning, I would stare at the goals on my vision board: 100,000 subscribers, a six-figure salary and becoming an entrepreneur. I was working towards all three at once and it was exhausting but I kept pushing on with the thought of what my life would look like once I had achieved these things and how positively I would be perceived as a result.

A few months later, I was holding my 100,000 YouTube subscriber plaque after launching my online jewellery store and getting on track to make £100,000 that year . . . yet I felt *nothing*. I celebrated myself for a day and was beaming with pride but when I woke up the next morning, I could only think 'what now?'. Life didn't feel different and I didn't feel any different either. The overwhelming sense of pleasure was nowhere to be seen and, instead, I was plagued by the stress of increased workload because I didn't feel satisfied.

This is due to a concept called arrival fallacy (named by author Tal Ben-Shahar), which explains that arriving at a certain point or accomplishment is anticipated to bring about long-lasting happiness, but in actuality, fails to do so. A common example of this is believing you will finally be happy when you get the dream house, make more money or win an award. I associated accolades with fulfilment and I couldn't have been more wrong. Although I felt lost for a few days, I learned a lesson that changed my life for the better – happiness is created, not found. I realised I experienced more excitement in the pursuit of my goals rather than the completion of them. Getting up every day to get one step closer, learning something new or acting in a way that would make my younger self proud was what left me going to sleep feeling accomplished, not an award or an amount of money.

When I attained those things, all I could think about was what I was going to work towards next. Don't get me wrong, money is important, and it can be a tool that opens the doors to new opportunities, but real happiness lies in experience and the journey there. How could you ever achieve self-love and self-confidence when you pin them to external factors like appearances, cash and status?

All the happiness and fulfilment you crave is already within your personal control and depends on your perception of yourself and of the world, the number of opportunities you believe to be available to you and the standards you think you need to attain to be deemed acceptable of love and kindness in society. You receive what you believe. If you go out into the world fearing you don't look the part or lack the skills, others will treat you accordingly. On top of that, your own actions will limit what you can achieve because if you lack confidence in something, your brain will sabotage you in the form of procrastination or negative self-talk to sway you from even trying, hence your reality always stays the same.

Similarly, if you believe other people will always be one step ahead, you'll never be in the headspace to think bigger. Self-love isn't only about affirming your beauty in the mirror every morning, it's about recognising your worth so you never compare yourself to your own detriment. It's about giving yourself your best shot and removing the obstacles that will prevent you from getting there. Imagine a reality in which you are unconcerned by the inner happenings of everybody else's life – exactly who you are and how you live then becomes acceptable because there's no other standard. There's nothing external to live up to.

You are capable of creating that reality through changing your consumption. We are the ones actively inviting comparison into our lives. I used to know too much information about everyone around me as well as influencers on the other side of the world. What they ate, how much money they made, what their weekends looked like and even what their relationships were like. This sent me on a downward spiral of self-hatred because I spent more hours in a day watching other people live their dreams rather than building my own. So, I switched it all off.

Today, my social media contains only things that make me feel good because *I made it* that way. I follow a limited amount of people and I only engage with accounts that inspire or educate me. As a result, my focus is on how I can enrich my day ahead because I'm oblivious to what other people are doing and it keeps me grateful for what I have. Obviously, there will still be rare occasions when I see celebrity news and hear of people achieving big things I've been aiming for, but my self-belief protects me from comparison. I use other people as walking inspiration for everything I can grasp.

Consider the world as your very own real-life Pinterest board, an opportunity to use comparison to your advantage. It can be a positive tool in self-growth when used for motivating purposes. When you surround yourself with people who are further ahead, it broadens your horizons and allows you to see your goals as more achievable. So, next time you see a young successful entrepreneur on your feed, save it and use it to fuel your own business plans, if that's what you're interested in. Jealousy is our brain trying to communicate the desires that will lead you down the path you were always meant for, and self-love will help you pursue that desire.

DOES YOUR ROUTINE FOCUS ON EVERYONE BUT YOURSELF?

Get up and rush to work, be nice to that co-worker you hate, come home from school to study some more, help your mum make dinner, respond to texts on time, walk the dog, go to the gym, wake up early to run that errand, plan something nice for your boyfriend, schedule time for your friends, look into getting another job, clean the house, check on your family, remember to network, post more online, start that side hustle, attend that party, read more books, help out more . . .

Among all the daily demands of life, how often do you truly have time to be alone with your thoughts? And I mean complete intentional solitude. It's not just about doing something alone like going to the grocery store or driving to work, it's about spending quality time with yourself without any agenda or need for achievement.

How can you feel confident when you haven't found your purpose because you're too busy pleasing everyone else around you? How can you expect to be full of self-love when your cup is always empty from giving your energy to every other area of your life? How can you effortlessly write a list of your favourite things about yourself when you haven't even had the time to recognise what those qualities are? Solo dates are so important because they provide this quality time. So activities like watching TV, facetiming a friend, writing a to-do list or scrolling through social media can't play a part. Solo dates don't have to be extravagant. You could sit in a café to people watch, you could take yourself window shopping, you could have a picnic in a park alone to clear your head. Whatever fills you up without the need for distraction so that you can finally pay attention to yourself.

We have been raised to prioritise commitment to others over ourselves but this can destroy us in the process. We give chance after chance to an undeserving ex, stay kind to unkind family members or neglect our own needs to be there for somebody else. Self-love means no one can take from you anymore. When you achieve complete serenity in who you are and lose all attachment to pleasing others, their control slips away. No wonder the practice of falling in love with yourself feels so strange. People will label you selfish, vain or self-obsessed. There's nothing wrong with putting your needs first, admiring the way you look or finally healing years of self-hate to discover how much there is to love about your soul and expressing gratitude for that daily. Not to mention, who else should your universe be centred around?

If you start taking care of your own needs, you become a happier and more fulfilled person who will then have greater capacity to help your loved ones without need for recognition or risk of resentment. But there are still people who choose to use this label to vilify you for not being the person *they* need you to be. We have to change the narrative around putting yourself first. It's about setting the highest standards for your life and then whole-heartedly committing to them, taking pride in cut-offs, not tolerating disrespect for the sake of company, being picky with the energy you choose to surround yourself with, not accepting people into your life because they like you but instead taking the time to assess whether they align with you. When you establish the treatment you wish for and you provide it for yourself, you will not settle for people who want your time without satisfying the standards you set to earn that access to you first.

When you focus on pleasing others, your entire life becomes a performance in which you must trade your authenticity for approval that is never guaranteed and will never bring you happiness, only temporary external validation, which becomes an addictive cycle as you place others' opinions above your own. When you give this power away, becoming overjoyed at someone's praise, you are inevitably made miserable the second you are insulted. Accepting compliments is important, you deserve them, but using them to define yourself and decipher your value is what leads to changing yourself for everyone else. Conversely, when you live for yourself, you only do things that help you achieve your desires, and suddenly your own approval becomes the most important goal of the day. Then, when someone attempts to criticise, you remain untouched because you were never concerned about their opinion in the first place – your self-validating attitude eradicates any effect of outside opinions.

I used to question my choices constantly in university because I didn't have that 'meet your lifelong friends' experience I was expecting. I started and ended several friendships, while my hometown friends remained surrounded by the people they'd met in freshers' week. It made me feel unlikeable and like friendship didn't come to me easily. Now of course I see that when I was judged by my peers or dealing with the aftermath of friendship drama, it gave me the freedom to be selfish. Being disliked was the most liberating feeling because there was no more approval to lose; I no longer had anyone's opinion to concern myself with.

So I leaned into the fact that I didn't fit in and I used it to my advantage. I started my YouTube channel with no fear of how I'd be perceived; I put myself out there and felt complete freedom to reinvent myself. I truly wouldn't be who I am or where I am today if I was liked by everybody because it would have put me into a box that I would have been too afraid to outgrow. I would have been so attached to the version of myself that was approved by everybody else that it would have constricted the possibility of who I could become.

WHAT DOES 'SUCCESSFUL' REALLY MEAN?

Standards of success are instilled and reinforced in us every day and one of them is the importance of romantic love and how it defines us. Have a date on Valentine's Day. Find your person in your twenties. Have a big wedding. Why aren't you married yet? I'm sure your time will come. Not to mention every movie that starts with a hardworking, independent woman who doesn't find happiness until a man comes to 'save her' from the life she built for herself. Even as little girls, we were taught that the romantic love in our life completes us and it will always come from another person. What they fail to mention is that this standard comes with a lifelong journey of comparison and chasing because you've been conditioned into *waiting* to feel happy and successful, even though you are the only person who has the power to control your feelings.

I believed the narrative I had grown up watching and so I became a serial dater from the age of 17. And by 21, as you have read, I had already been in four failed relationships. I had the fancy dates, the daily 'I love you's and someone to fall asleep with over the phone after talking all night, but all of that dopamine slipped away in each and every break-up. I was also consumed by regret at all the mistakes I had made in choosing the wrong partners and rushing into things, because it cost me time I could have used to get ahead with my personal goals. Chasing the ideal of being a girlfriend brought me more suffering than it did joy. It was an addictive cycle caused by my feelings of incompleteness in my single phases, which meant I would always be looking for the next person to make me feel loveable again.

So, I embraced my singlehood. I reframed my perspective and started to see it as a gift rather than something I desperately wanted to get rid of. I realised there was so much opportunity in living life on my own terms and that privilege could be taken at a moment's notice. You could meet your soulmate tomorrow and your entire life would change. Of course, it would be magical, but you would also lose out on the experience of being a single woman with energy, time and money she gets to expend all for herself. So why aren't you spending every day with that gratitude?

I used this new mindset to take myself on weekly solo dates. At first, it felt uncomfortable because I was thinking everybody's thoughts for them: I looked like a loner, I must not have any friends, everyone was laughing at me or pitying me or wondering why someone like me would sit in a restaurant alone. These irrational thoughts consumed me because of the shame that society projects onto those who are alone. But the truth is that those who look down on us for being alone are projecting the deep shame and insecurity they themselves would feel if they were in our situation. It is inconceivable to most people how someone could be completely content without a partner and so they make assumptions about the lack of fulfilment in your life based on their own limiting thoughts and life experience. They most likely attach their worth to another and define themselves based on the external factors, particularly relationship status. You can't blame them. When have any of us been taught how to find our confidence within ourselves? But you can understand that their opinions have nothing to do with who you are. All you can do is live in *your* authenticity.

I made it my mission to remove the negative connotations around being in a relationship with yourself. I'd be lying if I said it was easy. On Valentine's Day 2022, I was sat in a romantic low-lit restaurant drinking wine and eating dinner alone, beaming with pride that I had made such progress on my self-love journey and that I now had the confidence to sit in a room surrounded by couples. But it didn't take long before the waiter began questioning my decision and insisting all evening that I must be 'so sad'. My solo date turned into a pity fest, with every service interaction including a pouty face, kissing teeth and an 'aww' to try and comfort me on what he thought must have been a depressing day for me. My joy turned into discomfort and the thoughts of judgement slowly started to creep back into my mind.

Although it was a disappointing experience, I used it as motivation. I used exposure therapy (a CBT technique designed to help eradicate fears and anxieties by exposing the patient to the source repeatedly) to essentially become numb to the thought of other people's opinions and embrace my own feelings first. For me, this meant more solo dates in even scarier environments.

The point here is to be selfish. Make uncancellable plans and set standards for yourself that don't involve anybody else because that's how you build the foundation of a strong sense of self. When you know exactly who you are, you won't accept others' twisted ideas of you as truth. I went to a concert alone, I travelled to a different country alone and I celebrated my birthday alone. All these experiences forced me to listen more to my thoughts, to learn more about myself and to experience who I am as a person when I'm not interacting with other people. As a result, my self-perception is now unbreakable because no one could possibly know me as well as I do, to have a valid opinion of me. After all, I'm the one who has spent the most time with myself.

HIGH STANDARDS HURT

Lastly, let's talk about the difficulty of high standards. Not settling is hard but being 10 years deep in a relationship and realising you're not receiving the treatment you deserve is even harder. When you long for companionship and romance, it's easy to get swept up by the respectful guy or girl who always listens and makes you feel safe. It's easy to fall in love when they wine and dine you, shower you with compliments and open every door for you. It's easy to think they're the one when they show you off to all their friends and paint you the picture of a perfect future together.

But what if I told you that all this is the bare minimum? These acts are the foundation of forming a relationship and expressing care for someone. Romantic gestures are simply what separates someone from just being your friend, they are not indicative of your soulmate. Many of us can make the mistake of thinking we've found a high-value relationship when really we've just found another best friend to do fun things with and effortlessly talk to 24/7. That is an important element of a healthy relationship but certainty not the entire package. Real standards enter the picture when you start asking yourself:

- ☐ What do I want from this relationship?
- ☐ How can we grow together?

- ☐ Do they align with my values?
- ☐ How do I want to be treated daily?
- ☐ Are our goals compatible?
- ☐ What do I want our relationship experiences to look like?
- ☐ How do I want my partner to show up for me?
- ☐ Am I happy with the effort contributed from both of us?
- ☐ Have we discussed our preferred communication styles?
- ☐ Have we figured out a way of kindness out of conflict from this?
- ☐ Do we use our conflicts as opportunities to understand each other more?
- ☐ Are my needs consistently provided for?
- ☐ Does their day-to-day routine suit mine?

Choosing the right partner is about recognising you are not only investing in the person but in their lifestyle too. Your entire life will shift as a result of being with that person. Would you sacrifice the life you've been building in your head for years just to be with a person, if they don't match what you've always dreamed of? You could pick the most thoughtful, fun-loving and hardworking partner, and that could still be a betrayal to yourself if you love adventure and they always want to stay in, you want to live in the big city and they never want to leave their hometown, you imagine a life of luxury and they imagine one of ease. So, the next time someone tries to minimise the time it takes to find the right partner for you, remember that most people are more focused on the idea of having someone and how it looks to others rather than thinking much about whether they've done the best for themselves, their inner child and their future self in choosing that partner.

When you raise your standards, you will receive less attention, you'll remain quiet when your friends are sharing their wild dating stories – and at times, this will make you doubt your new lifestyle. The truth is that higher-value experiences are a trade-off to relatability and normalcy. Not everyone will like you but that's okay – you're not meant for the masses. You are intentionally limiting your dating pool to conserve your time for the things that actually benefit you. When you embrace this exchange and stay stubborn in your expectations, the universe will reciprocate in what it allows you to experience in life.

This is due to the law of attraction. This principle states that the life you experience is a result of what you think about, what energy you harbour and what experiences you tolerate. Author Vex King writes in his book, *Good Vibes, Good Life*, 'You'll only be able to attract what you want if you're able to maintain a positive mindset at all times. If you're in a negative mindset, you'll attract negativity and halt the positive manifestation process.' You have to be in the right environment for your energy to be reciprocated, whether it be physical or mental. I am now at a place where I see every daily decision as a test because it will determine what will come into my life next. For example, if a work opportunity comes across my desk, I will decline if it is below what I really want. When we accept what's below our value, we are telling the universe we are unsure of ourselves and we don't really believe we are worthy of our desires.

The silence in solitude can be uncomfortable if you have grown up in unpredictable and stressful environments, which often causes us to seek out this chaos in our adult life. We struggle to see the benefit of a peaceful life because we have been taught to wait patiently for the reward perceived as 'love' after a nasty fight or drama-filled day. We feel we must earn love through meeting the conditions set by another person. When you remove this toxicity, you may initially feel a lack of love and surge of loneliness in your life. But this isn't the case. You can choose to give that love back to yourself and this starts with shifting your perspective from loneliness to contentment in your alone time.

People are so addicted to their misery that a few days spent alone automatically translates to 'no one loves me'. In the beginning, the feeling of loneliness will frequently creep up on you and the comparison to everybody around you may be louder than ever. But imagine if you were thinking about yourself in this time rather than being so focused on the presence or actions of others. Loneliness is simply an attachment to all things outside of yourself. It's an inability to sit alone and a longing for someone/thing to distract you from the discomfort that is being alone with your mind. So, envision a mindset full of such positive self-perception that alone time becomes enjoyable. There is no loneliness to experience when you can sit alone contentedly because you love, support and care for you.

Your lifestyle will change significantly and you might find yourself alone at home on a Saturday night, looking down at your phone with zero notifications. The feeling of nothing to worry about is unfamiliar and so you'll create things to worry about . . . like FOMO. Fear of missing out is simply the result of uncertainty and insecurity in our lives. You assume you should be at the next place, with that friendship group, going on their holidays, receiving their blessings, to the point where you're blindly unaware of the blessings that are personalised to your needs sitting right in front of you.

This is why we focus on JOMO instead – the *joy* of missing out. This is when you have complete trust that you are exactly where you need to be with everything you could ever need in this moment to make your next ideal experience a reality. The assurance that life is not out to get you but is instead helping you every step of the way in handing you the lessons you need to become the person you have always desired to be. Everyone's lives will be different, and others might seem better, but they will never be aligned to yours. They might not need to set such high expectations or live your routines to meet their potential and that's good because they're staying true to *their* path. And now it's time you stay true to yours.

CHAPTER SUMMARY

- ☐ Society tells us what is good and bad, and this fosters our endless list of insecurities. Companies profit from changing trends and creating new standards of beauty. But beauty is subjective and for every positive opinion there'll always be a negative one to counteract it. So external validation is always cancelled out. Loving yourself gets easier when you choose a beauty standard that matches your natural beauty.
- ☐ Loving yourself gets harder with every new direction you get pulled in. How can you schedule time for yourself when there are friends to catch up with, parents to be there for, work tasks to excel in? It constantly signals to our minds that we come last in our own lives. When you wake up with the intention of making at least 50 per cent of your decisions based on what makes you feel good, you finally stop performing for others and start living for yourself.
- ☐ High standards protect you from low-value experiences. You might receive less attention or find yourself living an unordinary lifestyle, but you gain unordinary treatment in return. Following the actions and habits of the masses gets you average treatment. Take pride in your pickiness; most people are too afraid to think critically about their standards for fear of being alone.
- ☐ Letting yourself down will be a regular part of your journey. We aren't born knowing how to live life correctly and we will need to experiment travelling different avenues

in life. Some will leave us satisfied and some resentful. The latter is more important. You gain more clarity on the correct path with every mistake you embrace. So long as you keep focused on the strides of improvement you're making in your inner world, the appearance of your outer world won't matter as much.

CHAPTER HOMEWORK

- [ ] Create your own narrative of your beauty. Redefine one of your insecurities and make it into an affirmation you will repeat every morning for the next week: e.g. 'I feel great in my skin', or 'My features represent generations of beauty and they fit my face and my history perfectly'.
- [ ] Shift your consumption. Read magazines that reflect you, watch films that embrace your culture, create Pinterest boards about the qualities you struggle to accept. There are plenty of models and celebrities who own their unconventional body types and facial features – this normalises deciding how you want to feel about yourself.
- [ ] Schedule time this week to take back control of your routine, even if it's taking time getting ready in the morning before work, which helps me feel my best.
- [ ] Distance yourself from surface-level standards and use the list of considerations regarding relationships earlier in this chapter to get certain about the real standards you're seeking. How do you want to be provided for? What lifestyle do you aim to experience and what kind of person will match those ambitions?

CHAPTER 4:

TOOLS TO START YOUR SELF-LOVE JOURNEY

How do I begin the inner work?

Inner work is a conscious and active practice that encourages deep self-reflection and self-awareness to enable us to recognise our inner limits and how we can expand them to grow for the better. I believe that inner work is best achieved through the five components I break down in this chapter: energy and belief systems, fearless boundaries, self-perception, intentional joy, and discipline and accountability.

ENERGY AND BELIEF SYSTEMS

Let's start from the top: your mind, and what you feed it every day. We have to start challenging our limiting beliefs by understanding where they come from, such as social media, pop culture gossip, reality TV shows, past experiences and the people around us. Change the media you consume and alter the algorithm to have it work in your favour.

I found myself being drawn into the narrative that romantic relationships are bad and it made me mistrustful. This was no surprise since I was consuming media that focused on celebrity cheating scandals, break-ups and dating drama on television. I started associating the idea of dating with the disasters I had seen online and not only did it make me doubt whether there were any good men left but it lowered my standards. I was jumping for joy to find someone who was loyal, kind and romantic; I forgot that those qualities are the bare minimum foundation of dating somebody and there's so much more you can desire and get. There are so many healthy relationships in this world – couples who fall more in love every day, women who got everything they could have wished for and more – but no one focuses on that because it's not dramatic enough, so you have to force it into your world.

Once I recognised my limiting beliefs, I made a list and decided to intentionally consume content that challenged them. For example, I followed more couple content online, I watched healthy relationship lesson videos and I actively engaged with accounts in which people spoke highly of their love lives. I also muted content that caused me to doubt whether setting high standards was even realistic.

I would recommend going through your following list on every social media platform and doing a mass removal, only keeping those accounts that encourage you positively. After this, scroll through the explore page of each of these social media pages and click 'not interested' on the content that doesn't align with the highest version of yourself – e.g. celebrity gossip pages, Facetuned influencers, meme pages that keep you in scroll mode. Then type in key terms that align to your future self and engage with this content to get shown more of it on your feed – e.g. confidence tips, healthy dating advice, motivational videos, study aesthetic, productive vlogs. Searching for your desired terms on podcast platforms is another great way to change your mindset effortlessly while going about your day and learning new information. Replacing reality TV with self-help books will expose you to new and beneficial ideas that will help you grow.

Energy is sacred – unfollow and unfriend in real life. Feeling 'bad' for unfollowing or distancing yourself from someone is you solidifying a belief that other people's preferences are of higher importance than the energy you immerse yourself in every day, and therefore the life you experience. The friends you keep and the people you talk to affect your mindset and outlook on life, no matter what. I started with the simple task of stepping away from those who did not meet my standards for friendship or harboured negative energy that then seeped into my own. It may have made me lonelier, but it also gave me the chance to recreate my mindset as one that would allow me to attract a new reality with more aligned friends and opportunities. You can't accept people and things that don't serve you while wishing for better to come along: to welcome the new, you must let go of the old. It links back into the law of attraction. If you tell the universe that you identify with the lifestyle you currently have by continuing to accept it, how will you ever align with a different life?

But then I took it a step further. I have distanced myself from friends who I just loved and are still such amazing people, but who do not align with the life I crave. I realised that keeping them around makes me smaller. Being with people who aren't growing with you, and who always keep a certain image of you in their head, makes it harder for you to escape that version for yourself. To level up, you need to consume media or talk to people who can see your vision and encourage you to make a newer version of yourself. They are not attached to smaller and undeveloped ideas of you because they value your growth as a person over how you fit into *their* life. Plus, the wrong company will deter you from thinking big – I had friends in university who were so supportive, but they made such a big deal of my smaller achievements that it made me feel like I was doing big things when, in reality, I hadn't even reached half of my potential. Now I'm surrounded by people who congratulate me on my wins while acknowledging that I should go even bigger.

I would recommend widening your circle by meeting people in environments that align with your interests rather than making friends based on proximity and convenience, because it's very unlikely those friends will match the energy you are looking for. Searching for local events or networking opportunities is a great way to do this. There are also Facebook groups for women with similar interests and ambitions. Social media can be a good tool and it is supposed to connect us – so send a message to someone you admire or would like to be friends with. The worst that could happen is you don't get a reply, but if you don't try, you could be missing out on a friendship that has the potential to change your life for the better.

I only met my best friend a year ago and it was because she

sent me a DM on Instagram asking to go for lunch sometime. Her Instagram was so expressive of her personality and interests that I just knew we'd get along. Fast forward to now, I feel so grateful to have finally found the friend I had been searching for my entire life – someone who pushes me, understands me, teaches me new things, inspires me, holds deep conversations with me and shares a lot of the things that light me up – all because of a DM.

You can also change your mindset through visualisation. Visualisation is the practice of creating realistic mental images that allow us to watch and feel our ideal reality. Once you've removed the things that keep you stuck in the reality you no longer want, it's easier to start seeing yourself as the kind of person you desire to be. If your limiting beliefs cause you to doubt whether you're even worthy of your dreams or to be loved by the right people, simply imagining yourself having achieved those things can do wonders for your mindset long term.

As I mentioned earlier, the brain can't tell the difference between a real and imagined experience. Oprah Winfrey is a great example of this. The popular television host has said she overcame her childhood adversities by imagining herself as a successful talk-show host, seeing rounds of applause and the impact she would have on thousands of lives. She achieved all of this on the strength of her firm belief in this vision. The more vividly you think about something, the more likely your brain believes it's already happened, building new neural pathways that have the power to reprogram our subconscious beliefs and motivate new habitual behaviour, which in turn helps us in achieving those goals. For example, if your confidence is held back by a fear of how you are perceived, you can start imagining yourself in the specific environments where you will or have previously experienced that fear, but with the new outcome of feeling self-assured, having a positive impact on others and feeling immense gratitude for being exactly who you are. Conversely, the more you focus on your negative thoughts, the more you believe them to be true. So, for instance, if you feel nervous about presenting in class but replace thoughts of failure with mental imagery of clear public speaking, rounds of applause and a sense of achievement once you finish, this will improve your confidence for the task ahead and make it more likely too that your success in it will become a reality.

The more you expose yourself to the idea of your ideal outcome, the more likely you are to get it – if you start thinking people will like the way you're dressed, it shifts your body language as you walk into a room, which therefore makes you more approachable. If you start imagining having fulfilling interactions with others, you are more motivated to speak to them with intention, which makes you more likeable.

Though it's worth noting that of course visualisation can only get you so far. It's important to have a 'mental portfolio of proof' – a nickname I have given to the process of proving your limiting beliefs wrong and shifting your identity through your actions. So you call to mind when you have *done* things, not just imagined them. For example, it's far harder to struggle with fear of failure for too long when you are able to quickly reference two or three memories of times you tried something new and succeeded – it eradicates the self-doubting thought because you've taken action to prove its irrationality.

So, instead of letting your emotions guide and limit your behaviour, if you let this temporary fear motivate you to push past the fear and do it anyway, it will contribute to your portfolio of proof, which then removes the chance of feeling fearful another day. Let's say you're struggling with self-love because you constantly seek external validation and others' approval is a powerful determinant in how you feel about yourself. If you counteract this belief by intentionally doing something that will be perceived as embarrassing – whether it's posting the picture or wearing the outfit – you will find that nothing happens and you didn't need that approval after all. Free yourself by doing something cringe and you will realise your self-validation is good enough.

FEARLESS BOUNDARIES

Boundary-setting is unique to every person, but it includes making rules for what constitutes safe and appropriate behaviour in your relationships. For example, declining things you don't want to do or addressing your discomfort with the way you are being treated. People pleasing is the act of caring what other people think and trying to predict their needs or anticipate their reactions.

Psychologist Dr Juli Fraga says, 'When people perceive us in a way we don't like and can't control – for instance, after a relationship break-up – there is a temptation to over-compensate in other areas of life, to ensure people like us.' This is a common habit of those with low self-esteem, fear of rejection and trauma caused by being made to feel like you have to be perfect to have a chance at being liked. But you don't need to perform for others to be tolerable and you don't need to mirror their personality to be accepted.

The first step to building fearlessness is understanding the importance of being disliked. Living in your authenticity does carry more risk of judgement and rejection but it protects you from wasting time on friends who don't love you but rather a reflection of themselves in the act of your people pleasing. The more you expose yourself to the chance of being disliked, the more you filter out the people who are not meant for you and the easier it will be to find the tribe you are truly meant for.

People pleasing can also be a form of self-sabotage, when you force yourself into the wrong environments for the sake of acceptance from people who aren't even good for you. This links into fear. Setting boundaries with people feels scary because you are afraid of losing them or making a bad impression. But setting boundaries is a loving tool to ensure the growth and health of your relationships. If standing up for yourself and expressing your needs results in negativity or conflict, it represents the lack of accountability from the other person, not your wrongdoings. For example, communicating how you'd like to be spoken to in moments of conflict with your partner or family is real kindness so there is nothing to fear. It is you protecting that relationship from the risk of resentment or hostility and gives both parties the chance to grow and understand each other better, thus strengthening the bond. It also goes so much deeper than that: resorting to people pleasing for the sake of comfort and ease is you sacrificing the energetic vibration you operate at every day, to the detriment to all other areas of your life. Having this low vibrational energy reduces your success in attracting your desires, in showing up as your best self and even your physical energy as it causes sluggishness.

So how do we remove this? It's simple, by stepping outside of our comfort zone. The more you try new things, talk to new people and place yourself in new environments, the less you care about approval from others because you have the confidence and experience to know you can start over at any point. There's no fear of loss or rejection when you can always gain so much more. But this courage is only possible when you expand your world beyond your hometown, colleagues and immediate circle. When you do this, and you're meeting new people, you need to shift your attention to self-validation over external validation. Then, as your horizons expand, you realise how much abundance there is out there in so many different types of relationships, so tolerating disrespect from others is even less justifiable.

I used to make myself smaller in front of certain family members to avoid arguments or judgement. But all this did was teach me to become hyper-vigilant of other people's social cues and triggers, to anticipate their responses, instead of just being present in and enjoying my own life. Once I put myself in environments with new people, built better friendships and experienced others respecting my boundaries, it allowed me to clearly see those who I should no longer allow in my life – even if it was my own parent. I had previously seen myself as a very agreeable person; I thought setting boundaries was just kicking up a fuss until I learned I was really just living life on other people's terms. I was handing over the power of designing my own life to make everyone else's easier.

It's true that setting boundaries can feel uncomfortable and comes with the risk of losing people. I reframed my perspective to see it as a protection tool – it saves my time, it weeds out the ingenuine people from my life, it removes any needless suffering and allows me to live life on my most ideal terms. Boundaries are never something to feel bad about; if someone feels offended by you putting your wellbeing first then they clearly see your relationship as transactional, which is a problem.

The benefits of boundary setting are huge. It's the clearest green flag, knowing you're surrounded by the right people. Telling your partner you want to hold off on intimacy or communicating your preferences to a friend and being met with complete understanding paired with changed behaviour is the clearest sign of genuine care and reassurance. This is how you can know that you are finally surrounded by reciprocated effort and mutual respect.

Having an effortlessly enjoyable relationship with someone for so long and then suddenly needing to set a boundary can feel unsettling but I've found the perfect formula for this. This involves assertiveness in communicating and enforcing your needs, while maintaining respect for the other person. In this example, let's say I'm trying to set a boundary for more space within my friendship so I can maintain my independence without feeling guilty for not always texting or calling them:

- Start the conversation by disarming the other person so they don't feel like they're being attacked. This can be done through reassurance and affirmations: 'You know, I really appreciate our closeness and how comfortable I feel talking to you about everything. I'm so grateful to have found someone so trustworthy.' The opening softens the blow before you express your concerns. Your friend can then have this conversation with you while remaining confident that it isn't a personal attack.

- Now set the context for your boundary by explaining why you need this rather than why the other person is in the wrong: 'Life is getting so busy and I'm having to change around my priorities to focus more on my goals. So, I can't commit much time to texting and facetiming.' This will help build compassion and understanding in the moment and help the other person see why respecting your boundary is an act of kindness they can do for your friendship.
- After this, reinforce what you need to make it as clear as possible, which won't seem so scary because of the reasoning you've backed it up with: 'Sometimes I get overwhelmed by how demanding life is and I feel bad for not catching up with friends. Scheduled time to catch up weekly instead of random calls every day would make me feel more in control of my tasks and less guilty for being in my independent phase.'
- Lastly, finish on a positive: 'I would love to know what day we can commit for our weekly catch-up call or lunch date – what suits you best?' This cushions the boundary from feeling intense and makes the other person feel needed rather than abandoned. Which

they almost certainly would if you were to say, for example, 'I need you to stop texting me every day as it stresses me out.'

SELF-UNDERSTANDING

You can't love yourself if you don't really know who you are. When you don't take the time to form a comprehensive view of yourself, you will internalise the definitions everyone else makes about you – good or bad. Self-perception is the view you have of yourself and, despite spending every second of your life with yourself up to this point, your self-perception can become terribly distorted and inaccurate.

When I went to university, I was getting compliments, going on dates for the first time and making more friends than ever. People praised my appearance and style, and yet I still identified as and internally felt like the 15-year-old reject who wouldn't know confidence if it hit her in the face. Sometimes, you can grow and change and even do a complete transformation, but your self-perception doesn't catch up because you're not actively creating it. It stays stuck on past comments and experiences, which are completely irrelevant to the life you live now.

Perceiving yourself negatively will disrupt your potential and your relationships. Not only will you think badly about yourself, but you'll project that belief onto everybody else and, inadvertently, sabotage those relationships, particularly when others are viewing you through a lens of copious abundance, causing disconnect and futile misunderstandings.

The first step to consciously choose your self-perception is altering your past narratives to your advantage. Shadow work is the identification of your wounded self and unprocessed traumas. You can go into a past painful memory to confront parts of your inner world by questioning certain thoughts or habits. The aim is to comfort ourselves through learning how to fully love and embrace our 'flawed' parts rather than supressing and judging them. This practice is recommended to do with a therapist, especially in cases of severe trauma. In my experience this was a really useful practice when it came to processing difficult relationships.

One way to do this is by closing your eyes and vividly imagining a past memory that has caused a limiting belief in your present life. You need to see the exact environment in which it took place, what you looked like, where you were and what you were doing, until you're watching this past situation like a video playing in your head. When you can see it as clearly as when you experienced it, imagine your current self, with all your wisdom, new life and fresh outlook on the situation walking into the memory and approaching your past self. When you interact with your past wounded self, you comfort them, give them a hug, tell them what you wish they would have known. Show them who you end up being and how life gets so much better, even though it doesn't feel like it right now.

This lessens the impact of the event and replaces the limiting belief with proof of its irrelevance in your current life. It separates the past from the present, so you stop identifying with the wounded version of yourself because you're shown clearer than ever the new reality you've made for yourself. It also links into reparenting yourself – giving yourself the care and affection you may have otherwise lacked from primary caregivers. The purpose of this is to allow yourself the opportunity to adopt new ways of thinking and living, as well as establishing new standards of how you wish to be treated through giving yourself a strong foundation of self-respect and self-love that you may have lacked in childhood.

The second step is to consider how others have impacted your self-image. Write out a list of every insecurity or limiting belief you've harboured that was created by another person. After years of wanting a nose job, I'd had enough. I made the decision to love my nose rather than defining it based on someone else's opinion. I fought my insecurity with logic. Beauty is subjective and something that a million people love will also be hated by another million – it's impossible to please everyone so why should I change myself to be more acceptable to one person when I'll still receive rejection no matter what?

So I stopped associating asymmetry and a crooked shape as something bad but rather something that made me, me. My nose doesn't define me, it's not the first thing people notice about me, it hasn't kept me from all the blessings life has to offer, so why should it be such an important issue that makes me feel bad about myself? Once you've acknowledged the source you can start to use logic to challenge negative beliefs about yourself, replacing them with positive ones backed with evidence.

You can destroy limiting perceptions with logic over emotions by answering the questions overleaf:

- ☐ Why does that person's opinion hold more value than my own?
- ☐ Who shares this feature of mine that I'm so insecure about, and yet they embrace it? (E.g. body positive celebrities, models with a similar skin tone, influencers with similar personality traits.)
- ☐ Why can't I also create and accept a beauty standard that honours who I am as I am?
- ☐ What are three qualities that makes me uniquely me?
- ☐ What are three other qualities I'm grateful to have?
- ☐ Who would I be and how would I act if today was the first day of my life?
- ☐ What's holding me back from loving myself unconditionally? Why do I have to have those qualities to feel worthy? Who told me perfection is the only acceptable standard when it's impossible?
- ☐ What parts of myself do I judge the most? How can I be kinder to my younger self?
- ☐ What can you forgive yourself for?
- ☐ What can I forgive others for? Can I start to give them compassion and stop taking their actions personally, but rather as a sign of their unhealed self?
- ☐ Do I give my insecurity so much attention and importance? What are three other self-defining qualities that deserve more attention? (E.g. your energy, the impact you have on others, the life you've built, your humour, your impeccable taste, your self-expression, your compassion, your unique world view.)

- ☐ How has my self-image affected my relationships with others?
- ☐ How has my self-image impacted my daily decision making?

Once you've released past pains, it's time to get to know yourself. We spend so much time questioning others, engaging in deep conversations and trying to understand them, but how often do you give that attentiveness to yourself? Taking the time to understand every detail that makes you, you, means you won't believe everything others have to say about you. When you whole-heartedly understand every part of your personality – what there is to love, what you're worthy of, how your life so far has made you, you, what your character is, how you think, who you were, who you are and who you are growing into – you'll laugh anytime someone tries to make a false statement about you, good or bad.

Everyone views you through a completely different lens based on their own life experience and world view – no two people will ever look at you the same, not even your parents. Just how people's criticisms of you are automatically invalid, as are their compliments, as both are biased. The only accurate opinion of you is yours, because you are the only one who has been in your mind and has experienced every single second of your life. Once you recognise that and pair it with intentional self-discovery, any comment ever made about you will no longer be registered nor have the power to influence your self-perception. How do you get to this level of detachment and self-assurance? Through self-learning.

You can't love yourself if you continue the exact same behaviours and patterns of the self you despised. Shifting self-perception means doing something different to signal a change to your brain, so it no longer associates you today with the mistakes and traumas of your past. For example, by practising a morning routine that values high vibrational healthy habits like meditation and exercise over the comfort of scrolling in bed for hours. Another example is distancing yourself from triggers, like taking a break from dating for a while or spending your weekends in solitude instead of trying to keep up with your peers.

Of course, we aren't robots, we wake up with different energy levels and emotions every day and if we don't plan around that, we're setting ourselves up for failure and our self-esteem takes a hit consequently. So the changes we make come with compassion and understanding, and having the option of alternate routines. You're not supposed to be perfect and perform the same level every day, so as you're planning out your new identity shift, create a list of 10 ideal habits you'd like to perform every day. You can then use this as a menu and pick three or four that suit you, depending on your capacity for the day. Alternatively, you can plan ahead and create different routine options for high energy days, sick days, time-restricted days and rest days. Here's an example of my different morning routines:

High energy:

- ☐ 6am wake up
- ☐ Meditation
- ☐ One-hour gym workout
- ☐ Thirty minutes reading

- ☐ Journaling
- ☐ French class

Sick/slow days:

- ☐ 8am wake up
- ☐ Meditation
- ☐ At-home yoga

Rest days:

- ☐ 7am wake up
- ☐ Thirty minute walk to get coffee
- ☐ Deep-clean apartment
- ☐ Reading

This helps me feel more accomplished, makes a habit out of showing up for myself consistently, raises my self-esteem and reduces the need for perfection. Plus, habits like these are centred around focusing on yourself, raising your energy, hacking your happy hormones and building on a portfolio of proof. All of which contributes to the practice of loving yourself more. Your happy hormones are dopamine, serotonin, oxytocin and endorphins. Each boost your mood in different ways. For example, oxytocin is the love hormone that can be 'hacked' through hugging your loved ones or a pet, while dopamine (our reward chemical) can be hacked through completing your to-do list or trying something new.

Remove the phrase 'should be' from your vocabulary. It is dangerously easy to become filled with guilt when you're fixated on everything you *should be* doing – eating healthily, working harder, balancing friendships, going on dates, working out. You'll be so beaten down when you feel you should be but you haven't that it will compromise the motivation you would have otherwise had. Replace 'should be' with action. The second you want to do something, schedule time for it, incorporate it into a routine and hold yourself accountable.

I was constantly plagued by the idea I wasn't fulfilling my potential in work, so I spent a day researching income streams, healthy routines, work–life balance tips, procrastination tools and then put these new practices into my calendar to stay consistent. That way, there was no time for 'should be'. My life became an effortless system where every task on my to-do list was contributing to the things I always wanted.

INTENTIONAL JOY

Happiness cannot be found, it must be created. A state of joy and satisfaction is often attached to external ideas, but the truth is that nothing and no one can 'give' you happiness because it's really a conscious decision you must make within yourself. It is a series of difficult choices you take throughout your day with every moment you experience. It is the difference between a scarcity and abundance mindset. It is the shift from FOMO to JOMO and it is the assurance in your journey after you stop comparing. When you master the art of intentional joy, you start to love your life more and, unsurprisingly, that love is absorbed into you as a person too.

A lot of self-hating behaviours are rooted in jealousy, shame, guilt, sadness and fear – a joyful person is so immersed in embracing every moment of their reality that they don't spare a second to feel those emotions. This starts with removing envy and comparison. Embracing the joy of missing out comes from shifting your attention. Disregarding useless information about strangers' lives on social media by unfollowing and muting is a step in the right direction to prevent your curiosity from leading you astray. The same goes for intentional time away from your screen and scheduled time for solitude. Spending time alone is the easiest way to move your mindset away from jealousy to gratitude. The more you immerse yourself in living your life, the more you'll find to be grateful for.

Now that you've removed your distractions, you need to change your lane of curiosity every day and challenge yourself to find gratitude in your day. With this intention set, you'd be surprised how many otherwise unnoticed moments come into your view simply because you were looking for them, like sunsets, flowers blooming, children laughing, elderly couples holding hands, the warmth of the sun on your skin, the lunch you ate . . . the list is endless.

Now let's move onto cultivating an abundance mindset and releasing thoughts that foster a feeling of scarcity. This is about creating your desired definition of every moment. The difference between intentional joy and falling into the trap of waiting to have a certain lifestyle or be a certain type of person is subtle. The difference between how you approach situations is outlined on the next page:

SITUATION	SCARCE PERSPECTIVE	ABUNDANT PERSPECTIVE
Wanting to start a side hustle as a fashion content creator.	'This market is oversaturated and I'll have lots of competitors so I'll probably fail.' 'People will see me trying to become an influencer by posting my videos every day and it will be embarrassing when I don't get any views.' 'Why would the biggest brands want to work with me over creators with more followers and experience anyway?'	'This industry is booming and so many different people have found success in it! If they have created financial abundance and made their dream opportunities come true, that means it's possible for me too.' 'I have always been passionate about styling and I'm so grateful that social media makes it easier than ever to be discovered.' 'Even though so many people are creating similar content, no one is me! I'll always have my unique energy and fresh take on things. If I focus on letting my creativity and community-driven mindset push me forward, why *wouldn't* the biggest brands want to work with me?!'

SITUATION	SCARCE PERSPECTIVE	ABUNDANT PERSPECTIVE
Dating and trying to find the right partner.	'Trying to find the right guy seems so impossible these days. You can't trust anyone.' 'I don't know how to attract all the good guys – where do you even meet them?!' 'I need to reinvent myself and figure out my first-date strategy to get this to work out in my favour.'	'Having the freedom to date around and explore what I might like in a relationship is so fun! I get to embrace the gift of my singlehood and independence while ensuring I'm exploring all my options before I commit.' 'Whether I find my person next week or next year, I know it will all work out according to the timing that aligns to my life path. I'm enjoying myself in the process without needing to stress about controlling this situation – the right person will see my value and love me just as I am.'

SITUATION	SCARCE PERSPECTIVE	ABUNDANT PERSPECTIVE
At an event which will involve meeting lots of new people.	'I feel so anxious around these new people. Why is no one talking to me? I bet they're looking at me wondering why I look so awkward alone.' 'Am I too overdressed for this? Do I even fit in here? Should I have come in the first place?' 'Who was I kidding, thinking this might go well? I'm going to hide in the bathroom and scroll on my phone.'	'Turning up here alone was such a big step for my self-confidence! Even if I don't make any friends, just doing this one thing to step outside of my comfort zone is a massive win – I'm so proud of myself.' 'Looks like everyone's already made friends. I might as well introduce myself to give myself the best shot at growing my social skills.' 'I belong in this room just as much as everyone else here and my focus is only on the new opportunities I can grasp – how exciting!'

There is so much to be happy about when you simply shift the narrative of life within your favour.

DISCIPLINE AND ACCOUNTABILITY

Lastly, you need to be consistent in carrying out the practices and tools mentioned throughout this chapter. Implementing the following steps will aid you in staying on track throughout your self-love journey and finally putting yourself first above all else, as I've learned along my journey in doing so.

1. Motivation

Although it sometimes feels fleeting, motivation can be generated on demand if you think for your future self. You need to figure out your 'why', your purpose behind starting this journey in the first place. It will become your driving force. As Simon Sinek states in his book, *Start with Why*, 'All organizations start with WHY, but only the great ones keep their WHY clear year after year.' Although this is a business perspective, the same rule applies in remaining consistent on your self-love journey. It's the thing that pushes you forwards even when you crave the comfort of your previous life.

Many people disregard the time and dedication required to build and sustain self-love. If you picked up this book and decided to embark on this journey purely because it sounds good and makes sense to you to generally become a better person, you are more likely to give up. A better example of a driving force is tying this journey to your personal struggles. I set a bet with myself that I couldn't spend a year alone without running back to dating to chase validation. This was something I resorted to for years and felt deeply insecure about. I knew if I gave up on this journey, I'd have to face the embarrassment of not even being able to keep one promise to myself and proving all my insecurities to be valid. That fear was enough to keep me going.

For you, it could be setting the correct foundation which will help you thrive in all other areas of your life, like your career. It could be developing the right relationship with yourself to ensure you're dating the right calibre of people and no longer attracting toxic partners.

After you've set your purpose, it's time to prep for the hard days. I have motivational content ready that gives me the extra push when I need it: Pinterest boards full of quotes that remind me of why I started this journey, TikTok videos saved that remind me of the type of confidence I'm working towards, books with pages folded down so I can re-read the comfort and wisdom that once ignited the self-growth spark in me.

2. Documentation

This is another source of motivation as well as a crucial accountability partner in its own right. Tracking your progress throughout your journey not only serves as a daily reminder to show up for yourself but it also provides a wonderful net of comfort for the difficult days. In the times when you wonder if it's worth continuing, you will have access to endless proof of the days you felt better about yourself, the moments your insecurities started to shift, the experiences that created the new you, the lessons you learned and so much more. It will be your reassurance and your reminder to stay committed all in one.

You might choose to keep a journal and write about your experiences in a 'dear diary' form every evening. Or you can keep a video diary if you prefer. This is my personal favourite; I still go back to videos from years ago and I can see my energy levels and emotions that speak volumes about my progress without even needing to hear anything I was saying in that moment. This does such an impressive job at transporting me back in time to that specific moment, allowing me to live in it all over again and feel the growth even more intensely. A more romantic method is to write letters detailing your progress and learnings, dating them to be opened on specific points, such as a year from now, on your birthday, after three months of consistency and so on.

3. Weekly rituals

Set calendar reminders in your phone to remind you to incorporate your love languages in your self-care. For example, if your love language is gift giving, buy yourself fresh flowers or get your favourite latte from your favourite coffeeshop. My weekly self-love rituals are effortless habits now. For example, Sundays are always about hacking my happy hormones in the mornings, buying myself flowers, unplugging from devices, resting and engaging in self-care to feel my best and reset for a new week.

4. Daily habits

If your lifestyle doesn't allow for those weekly rituals, start with allocating time to the most important things. A simple shift from waking up right before you need to leave and rushing out the door to waking up just 10 minutes earlier to start your day on your own terms reinforces a lifestyle where you put your happiness and needs first.

5. Build patience

This is achieved by practising discipline in all other areas of your life. How you do one thing is how you do everything. If you show up in your goal of learning a new language with 50 per cent effort and inconsistency in practising each module, you are less equipped with resilience when self-love gets hard. Getting comfy with discomfort is the only way to master discipline – for example, going to the gym at 7am even when it's cold and rainy, introducing yourself in rooms that intimidate you and trying to do something that doesn't come naturally on a consistent basis grows courage. You build up your tolerance to discomfort so that the obstacles that once would have made you quit now feel like another regular step in the journey.

This was just a brief overview of the foundational actions you can start implementing to begin your self-love journey. In embarking on this journey you are bound to make mistakes, but every single step is a valuable chance to practise your self-love. Feeling bad when you mess up is pointless because failures are a crucial part of the self-love journey. You can't develop unconditional self-love without the bad days, so welcome them with open arms and shift your mindset away from 'I can't believe I did that' to 'what can this teach me and how can it help me grow the relationship I have with myself?'. Release your fear of not being able to keep up your new routine and accept the possibility that you will fail. In doing this, you will finally start the journey without letting negative possibilities hold you back, and in coming to face them, you gain wisdom. It's a win-win.

This chapter was designed so you can refer back to it often as you learn more about the concept of self-love. These actions can hold you accountable in ensuring you're still showing up for yourself while gaining new knowledge.

Aside from this, it truly all starts with healing, and part two discusses this in more depth . . .

CHAPTER SUMMARY

- ☐ Your belief system is affected by everything you come in contact with – unless you consciously challenge it. It can be supported through intentional consumption, such as reading books that allow you to inherit ideas that help your confidence or listening to podcasts that keep you motivated. Start doing things that challenge your limiting beliefs to prove your negative self-image wrong.
- ☐ Setting boundaries is the kindest act of love. It prevents resentment and gives the other person the chance to show their true colours and intentions. Neglecting to do so is an act of self-sabotage which leaves you powerless and at risk of keeping the wrong energy in your life.
- ☐ You have the power to create your own narrative about your life. This includes past painful memories, awkward interactions and discomfort within yourself. It all boils down to shadow work and choosing a self-perception that suits how you wish to feel.
- ☐ Happiness is created, not found. It comes from the choices you make every day and how you define everything you come into contact with. It's the difference between an abundance and scarcity mindset.

CHAPTER HOMEWORK

- ☐ Energy is sacred. Go about your day while identifying the triggers that keep you in modes of comparison or low energy. Remove consumption, people or habits that don't align to your highest self. Fire ruthlessly: your self-love is at stake.

- ☐ Write a list of the self-hating beliefs that are keeping your confidence small and then schedule tasks to do each day which will make them all invalid. E.g. 'my acne makes me ugly' translates to the action of posting unedited selfies, making eye contact and speaking to people while knowing the bumps on your face do not define you.
- ☐ Use the boundary setting formula outlined in this chapter to practise fearlessly saying no and prioritising your desires with someone this week.
- ☐ Answer the self-perception questions to start maintaining more positive opinions about yourself and understanding how you may be holding yourself back from living as your most confident self.
- ☐ Create three different routines that honour different energy levels you may experience so you still get to feel accomplished and maintain positive self-esteem even on days when your energy is low.

PART TWO:

HEALING

Everything is hard before it's easy

CHAPTER 5:

PUTTING THE PIECES BACK TOGETHER

What does healing look like?

Healing is chaotic, messy, emotional and downright uncomfortable . . . but every single second is worth it. It's not an event, it's a journey, and it is far from a straightforward one. You will find yourself going in circles, repeating the same mistakes, taking one step forward before taking three steps back. And all of this is normal. There is nothing mysteriously wrong with your ability to change. The irregularity in healing is a necessary part of the journey *everyone* must encounter to have fully learned the lesson. So, every time you think you 'messed up', you're actually checking yet another box in this process to becoming a better, wiser and stronger you.

There are many misconceptions that keep people from truly healing. The first is that it requires isolation. You do not need to be alone in this process. Life is not a perfectly clean white box with predictable stimuli, inside which you have complete control over your surroundings. In reality, you will have annoying co-workers, misunderstandings with friends and triggering familial conflict – and it is in these messy moments that you learn the most about what holds you back and what coping strategies could push you forward.

Male validation was at the centre of my healing journey. I had to distance myself from the male gaze to focus on the opinion I had of myself instead. This doesn't mean everyone needs to abandon their dating life to love themselves. I think challenging yourself to stay in the environments that trigger you while implementing new changes can lead to the most fruitful leaps in self-growth. For example, someone suffering from an anxious attachment style (the constant need for reassurance, feeling love has to be earned, suffering from jealousy, always needing to please) may benefit greatly by dating while consciously communicating their needs, creating a routine that makes their independence the centre of the universe rather than the relationship, and working through their jealous tendencies as they come about while caring for this person.

It's like break-ups. Getting over someone is easier when you never see them again and you just have to face the fallout of your emotions, but what if you ran into them tomorrow? And they were on a date with their new significant other? And they came over to talk to you?! How healed would you be then? Would the feelings come rushing back? Would nostalgia take over? Would you fall back to the version of yourself you were in that relationship? You never truly know you're over someone until you can look them in the eyes again and feel . . . *nothing*. Or rather, pure bliss, acceptance and detachment in knowing everything happened for the best. That's how healing works – you have to implement your new mindset among your triggers to make real progress.

Another myth is that healing requires you to rid yourself of negative emotions and memories. You're not supposed to be happy all the time. The gift of the human experience is to experience the full spectrum of human emotions. You shouldn't punish yourself for reacting according to how you feel. You deserve to feel your sadness when you're grieving the loss of someone you loved so deeply or angered when you are disrespected. The goal with healing is to remove the hold your emotions have over you. You get to decide when and for how long you feel your feelings, rather than feeling powerless and neglecting your real life to stay in a state of pain.

I find crying to be so healing. I will allow the tears to flow at the smallest of situations if I can feel them building up – I feel so free and light, like I just released all the tension and stress that was building up. It doesn't make me weak or sensitive. Many of us are put on these healing journeys after being taught to supress our emotions to the point we strongly believe it makes us undesirable and pathetic. The people who have made you feel as though your emotions are unacceptable are those who were once told the same and internalised that belief so strongly that they project it onto others and feel triggered by people's ability to stay in tune with and express the full range of their emotions. People can only meet you as far as they've met themselves. Don't take their 'sensitivity' insults seriously when they're caused by a lack of self-love and compassion within themselves. Of course, they don't understand why you treat yourself with such kindness when they're used to performing to make everyone but themselves more comfortable.

You're not on this healing journey to 'fix' yourself or become perfect. You're trying to do these small favours for yourself each day to remove the triggers, limiting beliefs and uncontrollable emotions so you have a greater capacity to see the joy in the mundane moments, rather than allowing your experiences to be tainted by your continuous perception of all that is bad. An unhealed person argues with their partner and starts to question the relationship, their worth and their partner's intentions. A healed person has the same argument with their partner and naturally feels hurt but they understand that there is no love without conflict. They can see the joy in the ability to cope and grow through that pain point with their partner so they can understand each other better and create an even stronger foundation for the relationship.

Healing has no fixed timeline. It is lifelong and you can find yourself confronted with difficult feelings a year after you thought you fixed it. This still happens to me and I am always pleasantly surprised by it, instead of using it as an excuse to feel bad about my incompleteness. I really feel gratitude that this has come into my awareness because I'm excited for who I'm about to be once I work on it. Having a bundle of good days followed by a bad week again does not negate your healing – it provides a chance to reinforce what you've learned. The bad days are tests from the universe. If you resort back to your old ways of coping, you will then be presented with the same lesson in the form of different people and environments over and over again until you learn the lesson.

Despite each of my ex-partners in my four back-to-back relationships being so different, they all served their purpose for me to learn my pattern of settling for less than I deserve. I tried to start my healing journey after my second failed relationship, but I failed by jumping into the world of casual dating. This happened again after my third break-up, when I spent three months alone before finding myself in a committed relationship once again. I failed my tests. But when I started my self-love year in 2021, after six months of consistent progress, I was approached by a man who was exactly my type and was eager to plan an extravagant date day with me. This time, I observed him closely and recognised his attempts at love bombing me. I saw the red flag in his urgent pursuit and immediately blocked his number. My first passed test!

Another six months of smooth-sailing self-love followed this victory until I become fast friends with two girls. Their enjoyment of putting me down slowly became very clear. They often teamed up in giving me backhanded compliments or making fun of my interests. Despite this negative energy, I stayed. I had always struggled with female friendships and I didn't want to walk away from yet two more of them. It wasn't until I found out that they had been talking behind my back and lying to my face that I finally had the courage to walk away. I felt ashamed that I even let myself get into this situation. While reflecting, I discovered that this experience was my responsibility. I hadn't created the necessary boundaries to protect myself from bad friendships like I had in my dating life, and it stemmed from my deep insecurity around lacking close female friendships. This one realisation allowed me to shift where I was looking for friendship, identify the green flags I desired and start putting myself on the pedestal in these interactions. I stopped accepting friendship for the sake of it but instead spent more time observing whether people were good enough to have access to my energy.

I am so thankful for that lesson because it led me to my current present moment. I have a close-knit group of closely aligned, positive friends who have been in my life for two years and shown nothing but love and support. I truly wouldn't have found the type of friendship I've always dreamed of if it wasn't for the repeated hurdles that were thrown at me. They were nuggets of wisdom the universe was offering to help me get onto the right path with the right mindset. There's no such thing as failing on this journey when every mistake will transform into newfound mental resilience. I look forward to the time I fall over because I know a positively life-changing revelation will always follow.

Many make the mistake of believing healing equals being the best version of yourself. Wrong. You become a new version of yourself, but this new version is a more authentic representation of who you've always been. It's not trying to be someone else, it's coming home to the truth you've always denied. It's looking inward and giving love to the parts you tried to neglect in pursuit of acceptance from others. With every new lesson and journey I've embarked on, I've uncovered new parts of myself that help connect me to my younger self more than ever. It makes me stronger in living authentically, feeling confident without the need for change, being more fearless in my desires and embracing the process of making mistakes rather than feeling bad for making them in the first place.

Rejecting this process of repeat learning is a sign of your fear in facing your true self. Only those who have started the work in healing truly come to appreciate the satisfaction of facing each lesson and how liberating it feels to confront what has felt so heavy in your heart all these years. Healing is an exciting journey and once you start, it's unlikely you'll ever wish you were just 'done'. Desiring normalcy is a loss and overrated – wanting to be like everyone else will send you 10 steps back because you are abandoning your true self for external validation once again. We are set on unique paths to get above average results. But we can also be tricked into thinking we're at a loss because we are so used to seeing one type of life when we're really looking at the masses. Our journey of struggle sets us apart from the ease of being average and instead can lead us to living extraordinary lives because of the development we gain in the process.

Healing is the process of regulating your emotions after painful events disrupted the journey you were once on and the person you once were. You yearn for how things used to be, but trauma can make you lose yourself and alter the perception of all that you once knew. So it's about becoming the healthiest version of the person you have become *post* struggle. Healing must take place to move forward, instead of staying stagnant, wishing you could undo what happened to you. Instead, it's about taking that experience and growing from it, developing a new mindset that protects you from making the same mistakes again. It's about removing the masks and false layers of self you have held onto out of fear or conditioning from other people and replacing them with the search for your authenticity.

It's possible to break down the process into 10 stages. After experiencing this time after time, I've realised the most appropriate solution to pair with each stage to progress past it.

THE 10 STAGES OF TRAUMA AND THEIR HEALING SOLUTION

1. Self-blame and self-education

Escaping toxic family members leaves you with little to no confidence, often due to gaslighting or emotional invalidation. Gaslighting is a manipulation tactic used to make someone feel unsure of their reality and sense of self, as explained by author Dr Robin Stern, whereas emotional invalidation is dismissing someone's feelings as being unimportant or not deserving of any attention. Plus, finally recognising the trauma you were put through after months or years of denial can cause you to feel stupid for not seeing it earlier. You feel partly responsible for your pain because you kept going back for more or waited for someone so incapable to change. When toxic situations affect your ability to thrive in all other areas of your life and maybe in your other relationships, you can't help but be filled with guilt. Even if you made the same mistake 500 times, you did not deserve what happened to you.

However, while you may logically know this, it can be hard for emotions to catch up and this is what self-education is for. It's important to gain awareness of your story and the real causes of it so you don't sabotage the rest of your life feeling mistrustful of your choices. I've read countless articles and books, listened to podcasts and watched videos to learn about narcissism – the signs, causes and effects. It had freed me from tormenting myself for enduring that behaviour because I finally recognised how impossible it was to avoid it. Learning about manipulation tactics, breadcrumbing, dysfunctional family roles, emotional abuse, trauma bonding or emotional unavailability will allow you to detach from taking the situation so personally. You can instead gain assurance in the fact that this person is stuck in their own trauma and can't help but treat everyone they come across accordingly. That is simply *their* reality, it never had anything to do with you. You start to view them simply as another part of your story instead of something to define yourself by, and that way you can finally progress past shame.

2. Sabotage and accountability

Self-sabotage is when you unconsciously (or sometimes consciously) create problems or obstacles within your life that prevent the fulfilment of your goals and successes. In my opinion, it happens when you are living from a place of comfort and familiarity, but when you're on your healing journey, you're supposed to remove yourself from the things that keep you in the vibration you experienced during your trauma. We chase familiarity because it feels safe even if that familiarity is rooted in chaos and toxicity – we desire its predictability. Returning to the vibration of your wounded self can take shape in something as small as listening to the same sad songs, watching the movies your ex loved, rereading texts, stalking ex-friends on social media and looking back on pictures from that time. These small habits are what led you down the path of taking the biggest backward steps in your healing journey, like texting your ex again or looking for help in all the places that do more harm than good.

Missing what once hurt you isn't a sign to give it another chance. It is normal to feel sad after making the right decision because choosing the path for your future self will separate you from what you've always known; choosing to go back to the past is simply a natural instinct because our brains are hard-wired to seek out comfort. The solution to this is to acknowledge help over harm. It's crucial to understand the difference between reparenting yourself by recognising and meeting your own emotional needs and retraumatising yourself by abusing quick dopamine fixes that make you feel better in the moment but also prolong the entire healing process.

Accountability is all about taking a step back to be honest with yourself and view your actions without complex emotions attached to them (which often leads us into the trap of justifying toxic patterns). All it takes is the ability to see the role you play in your obstacles and the solutions will naturally find you. More often than not, it's the denial we hold and the external viewpoint we fixate on that leave us blind to the power and control we have over our own lives.

I took accountability for my self-sabotaging tendencies and blocked my ex on every platform instead of complaining about his unsettling reappearance in my life; healing my attachment style through self-education instead of carrying on with the mindset that got me into the situation I was trying to escape and detoxing myself from the lifestyle I was used to so I could build up the highest tolerance for new environments in the long term. See the difference?

3. Guilt and vulnerability

We often tend to run away from processing our emotions fully because we feel guilty about what we feel and how long we feel it for. You know logically that someone was bad for you or that you made the right decision to leave a harmful situation so you should be happy, yet you find yourself feeling devastated for losing the thing that was bad for you. You feel so angry with yourself that you can't just detach and forget all about them. But why would you? Detachment isn't about negating all your negative emotions and it most certainly isn't about shaming yourself for missing someone years after the break-up. Detachment is the process of viewing your emotional reactions objectively instead of taking them as truth, because more progressive healing takes place when you start to observe why you might be feeling a certain way and what could be causing it, rather than trying to avoid the emotion altogether.

When you carry the emotional weight of shame and guilt, you are physically harming yourself. Continuing to stay in high-stress situations or entertaining negative thought patterns can make you physically sick. This emotional state can disrupt the body's hormonal imbalance, damaging our immune system and triggering our brain to release chemicals which can affect our health. That is why working on your mindset is such an integral part of self-love. If you would do anything to protect your child from getting sick, why wouldn't you give yourself the same treatment?

Embrace your suffering so you can be done with it. During the process of allowing your emotions to come out in their entirety, ask yourself what instances caused each of those emotions. What (not who) could help soothe this distress? What experience could you grasp now to create some comfort in your life? What did this experience teach you about yourself? How is it shaping your perception of love or life? Who do you wish to become after this? How will it change you for the better?

Everything changed for me when I stopped beating myself up for crying and instead started celebrating my sensitivity and ability to feel so deeply. While I hurt over the loss, I also expressed gratitude for getting to love in the first place. I recognised the lack of boundaries and self-worth that got me stuck in that place and used that realisation to forge a path to a better future instead of regretting what I wished I could have done before.

4. Curiosity and closure

Curiosity can drive you crazy – wondering why things ended up the way they did, all the possible alternative endings that could have happened, questioning if you should have done something differently or if you simply don't know the full story. It forces you to live within a reality that no longer exists, yet allows you to experience these emotions so intensely all over again that it stimulates the urge to go back for more to find out the answers. I've found myself most curious in nostalgia – which is dangerous as it can disguise every reassuring truth for your healing with a romanticised memory of every good time until it tricks your brain into justifying every mistreatment you were put through.

But nostalgia dies the more you live in the factual evidence. Gaslighting, dependency and manipulation are hardest to escape when your only truth is the one your abuser provides. This is why it's important to create your own closure. With every painful memory you can conjure up you must note it down to create your self-validation log. This is a document you keep listing every bad thing that happened or justified reason as to why you had to start this journey. It serves as your motivation and strength during times of weakness when nostalgia threatens to take over and undo your hard work in moving on. It acts as a barrier to prevent past manipulation by making you question yourself and feel the need to seek out closure when every single painful emotion they caused you is closure enough.

5. Manifesting pain and manifesting power

You attract more pain into your life the more you accept it as a part of your identity. Your trauma doesn't have to affect your forever, it can be a distant memory and a tool that aids you in building your dreams. It starts when you let go of the comfort you find in fetishising your sadness, like when you consume content that validates your victim mentality and encourages you to stay in a phase of hurting over healing. Your mindset is the key to making the shift from attracting the same reality repeatedly to using it as a tool to level up.

For example, Person A listens to heartbreak songs all day, complains about their situation any chance they get, searches for sad quotes online and uses their bad dating past to generalise relationships overall until they lose hope and lower their standards because 'true love is too hard to find'. On the other hand, Person B takes the time to experience their feelings fully, they journal to release each emotion, they learn about their situation through self-education and they reach out for support. Although this break-up has taken a toll on them, they're determined that it will be the reason they will find the right love one day. After all, every heartbreak brings you one step closer to finding your forever person. So, in the meantime they reflect on the red flags they identified in their past relationship and draw up a list of what this experience taught them and what standards and boundaries they will set in place to ensure an improved experience the next time around. They no longer associate with their pain – it's simply something they are learning and growing from. This journey has inspired them to learn more about the art of solo dating, achieving goals and creating happiness so they don't make the same mistake of making another person the centre of their universe ever again. So they shift the types of books they read, they invest more time in growing their female friendships and they take up hobbies that move them closer to the type of person they've always wanted to be, instead of the type of person they're so used to being.

6. Expectations and new narratives

Expectations are the root of all misery. That's not to say you shouldn't have any in the first place, but rather perfect the art of knowing when to let go of the expectations that are no longer serving you and moving towards a more aligned mindset that does. That way, you're not constantly reminded of your disappointment and loss but rather your abundance in all other areas of your life.

For example, I have suffered in dealing with my parental trauma for years. It's been this big gaping wound I've never quite known how to close. I always fixated on the treatment everyone else gets from their parents, the unfairness of my situation and the bare minimum every parent meet. But these expectations only deepened my misery, and they constantly reminded me what I lacked in a situation that could never be changed, despite my many attempts. So I tried to change the way I looked at these circumstances instead.

Why do I upset myself by continuously trying to get the treatment I desire from people who have shown time and time again they are incapable of providing it? If an expectation does nothing but cause me further grief, then why do I hurt myself by holding onto it? So I decided to create a narrative that would make me feel better instead. I looked at the situation as an opportunity to become my own support system and build a stronger relationship with myself instead of fixating on those I have lost. It's not fair and it's not the ideal situation, but it does release all resentment for my own sake. This is about taking ownership of my happiness again.

I stopped taking other people's actions personally and saw the root causes for them. My parents are just as complex, emotional and unhealed as anyone else; they have their own set of insecurities and limiting beliefs that hold them back and they are figuring life out just like the rest of us because it is also their first time living through it. That doesn't justify their neglect and mistreatment of me but it does liberate me from internalising their actions as an indicator of my worthiness and effort.

7. Reliving and releasing

Unhealed trauma is like a recurring nightmare, only it attacks you at any given moment. It's hard to just 'forget' what happened to you. Unhealed trauma can show up as unexpected emotional outbursts, panic attacks, irritability, avoidance and self-sabotage, to name a few. Even when you've moved on, seeing one thing that reminds you of a person from the past, hearing a song or seeing a similar situation can open up that wound again even wider. The reason this happens is because of emotional suppression. We are so eager to move on from our pain that a lot of it is often undealt with and unprocessed. The more you hold it inside of you, the more vivid the energy and experience will remain and pour out at the most inconvenient moments. Whereas voluntarily reliving your trauma allows you to release it on your own terms.

Releasing rituals can help take back control of your feelings. You are planning for the time you decide to pour your heart out and let your tears fall. During those emotional moments, you can grab a journal or digital diary to write out every single thing you feel. Rip the pages and note down every bad word you've been holding inside. Alternatively, screaming your heart out and acting as your own therapist can be a good way to not feel pressured by the presence of another person and you can freely rant and communicate your feelings into the world. The more you allow the pain you carry inside to come out of you through writing or talking, the quicker you can remove this negativity.

8. Uncontrollable anxiety and intentional peace

Feelings of isolation and betrayal can fester and taint our perception of everything around us. If you have started your healing journey feeling anxious, unlovable and unsupported as a result of how another person has treated you, it is now your responsibility to transform that belief so your current life doesn't fall to pieces because of the after-effects of that pain.

When someone hasn't responded to your text in a while, your traumatic past creates an automatic thought process that you must have done something wrong and you're going to be alone all over again. You prove your limiting beliefs to be true the more you allow its corresponding action to exist unchallenged. Whereas, when you pair it with an action like reaching out to a friend for advice and comfort, the irrational thought becomes invalid. You must force yourself to reach out and communicate to create a new habit loop to change that initial anxiety into a peaceful fix. Though this often won't come naturally because these intense irrational thoughts are built into our nervous system as a result of our negative past experiences that have shaped who we are and how we feel about ourselves.

When you experience anxiety, your heart races and your mind becomes frantic. When your fight or flight instinct has been activated repeatedly during a traumatic period of your life, it can result in your nervous system becoming dysregulated, causing intense emotional spirals and stress signals, even in a situation that doesn't on the surface seem like it would be that challenging. You can shift this seemingly uncontrollable experience to one that brings you peace instead through 'parts work'. Psychologist Dr Arielle Schwartz explains, 'Even though you are ready to heal, there might be a part of you that interferes with the process in an attempt to protect you from vulnerable feelings that feel threatening to your sense of self.' Parts work starts with recognising the self that brought about this limiting belief and the timeline that part of you represents. For example, recognising that the social anxiety you currently experience stems from the part of yourself that felt repeatedly rejected and isolated by peers as a teen. Once you have a clearer image of this part in your mind, you need to carefully observe it while letting go of the pressure to change it. In this moment, you can stop identifying as that wounded part of yourself and instead disconnect to choose how much attention and energy you are going to commit to that part.

Just through these methods you are already taking steps towards self-accepting by recognising that part of yourself without any judgement. Finally, it's time to transform your triggers and create a peaceful relationship with this part of yourself. You can do this through journaling to reflect on what this part might need and what it is lacking. For example, answering prompts such as 'When did I learn this limiting belief and who was I at that time?', 'How have I evolved on my journey since that point in my life?', 'What would I tell that version of myself now about that belief?'. Asking these questions can start the process of disconnecting your past selves while building compassion and acceptance for them.

9. Denial and acceptance

Throughout the journey of healing, you will be confronted with denial because it serves as a soothing escape from uncomfortable emotions. But true healing can only take place when you fully acknowledge every event and truth of the person or situation, no matter how difficult it might feel. Denial doesn't mean being unaware of what happened to you. You can acknowledge that you have to heal yet tend to overlook the full truth of the events. For example, painful memories of a betrayal may be supressed, or perhaps you recognise that betrayal and the denial takes the form of justifying why it happened or minimising the impact of it. That means you can avoid having to change your perception of the reality and person you thought you once knew and trusted.

When you are confronted with new information that undermines the confidence you had about your understanding of a situation, it can negatively impact your self-esteem and trust, so denial is often used as a coping mechanism. But living in denial means we can't do something about these feelings and therefore we are stuck in our trauma long after it happened. So how do we reach acceptance?

For me, it always starts with self-education. I never truly understood the magnitude of my experience with narcissistic abuse until I read up on it to the point where I could no longer ignore it. The same goes for those suffering in toxic families or bullying. Researching what causes this behaviour in people will allow you to see the truth in your story more clearly. I then revisited that past relationship now that I had all the facts. Rereading text message and recalling arguments I had written down in my self-validation log suddenly all had a completely different story. It was overwhelming to see how I could have been so wrong and blind to the red flags, but I soothed this discomfort with self-compassion.

10. Going back to normal and creating a new normal

We all feel the desire sometimes to go back to how our life used to be before the events that broke us. Unfortunately, you can't go back in time and you can't attempt to manifest a reality without a particular experience because you are then denying yourself the growth that comes from it, choosing to stay stagnant within past comfort instead of facing your future. Going back to normal is overrated. If you attempt to continue as normal in the environment your trauma was created in you will constantly feel like there's a missing part of your reality. This will intensify the feelings of missing the person or environment you cut out for our own good because this 'normal' life now feels so unfamiliar without them.

To successfully move on, you can't identify or associate with that lifestyle; you must separate yourself from what feels so familiar, whether it be a place, a group of people, a morning routine or a mindset, and replace it with a new one. It could be as simple as walking a new route home every evening or changing your wardrobe – these things signal a shift to a new phase of your life. The more you continue implementing new habits and ways of living, the harder it gets to miss someone who wouldn't even know the new version of you and who you would never tolerate in this improved phase of your life.

There is always a way out, no matter what you're going through. Once you've changed the narrative and been through these common stages, you will be equipped to embark on your healing journey using the methods listed below . . .

HEALING METHODS

Shadow self

Healing starts with honouring your 'dark side'. We all have parts of ourselves that we neglect to acknowledge because of shame and insecurity, but true healing cannot take place until we love those parts of us too. This is known as the shadow self; it's the part of you that you can't fully see because you assume it's bad, but this rejection fosters further triggers and insecurities. This is why shadow work is used to gain complete self-acceptance. You can't expect to love yourself when you continue to punish yourself for the things you were shamed for by other people. For example, if you were rejected for being too shy or punished for being outspoken and you continue treat yourself as if you deserved this. The shadow self can be seen through the jealousy and judgement of others.

There's a stark difference between disliking something and feeling sufficiently bothered to impart judgement onto it. The reason for the latter is we only feel triggered by people who have what we desire, otherwise we'd feel indifferent to their actions. This isn't necessarily about your childhood trauma but rather the resentment you hold for those who are able to do the things you were/would have been rejected for. When you have not completely accepted your shadow self, seeing other people living openly with the qualities hidden in your own shadow feels wrong – you're so used to rejecting those parts in yourself and so you see others with those parts as inferior. You feel angered by someone's actions because they challenge your shadow self.

For example, judging how another person is dressed reflects the judgement you would have for yourself if you were to express yourself in the same way because you were taught it is undesirable and you would be rejected for doing so. Or you dislike someone for setting a boundary because you have disowned your own right to do so and instead live through your people pleasing tendencies. The shadow represents a deep dislike for a quality within yourself, whether it be in the area of expression, confidence, personality, lifestyle or emotion. To start combatting these triggers and giving those qualities the love and acceptance they so desperately need, you must build an awareness of your reactions throughout the day.

Having an evening journal practice is so useful for this because you can start to hold yourself accountable for the moments that triggered envy in you and start to question the cause of this until you uncover your shadow self. Once you understand what brought this rejection about, you can start the process of accepting this quality as another normal part of yourself that is just as worthy of love as the rest of you.

I used to find certain online content 'cringey' or pass judgement on certain people trying to put themselves out there in their authenticity. I assumed it was because I disliked that creator or what they were posting. But instead of simply scrolling on, I found that it really annoyed me. It wasn't until I understood the shadow self that I could recognise that what I was so bothered by was really mirroring a part of me that I refused to accept. I was dealing with so much insecurity and shame around my own authenticity at the time that I couldn't imagine putting myself out there online without needing to change myself to be more likeable. Seeing others exist so confidently without fear of rejection represented the kind of self-love I could have only wished to have at that point.

Once I realised where this annoyance came from, I had to start actively accepting that part of myself every time it was challenged. The next time I saw that type of content, I began to practice seeing the good in it to teach myself that it was okay to let that part of myself come out too. The majority of the time, judgement has nothing to do with the person you are judging and everything to do with the discomfort and rigid standards you hold for yourself. It's important to observe these moments so that you can rework these inner beliefs to make you more confident.

Shadow work

Shadow work is the process of exploring and questioning your limiting beliefs until you get to the root of your repressed traumas, fears and thoughts. This practice is recommended to do with a therapist, especially in cases of severe trauma. The purpose is to integrate your shadow self and shift your limiting beliefs into ones that benefit and uplift you, so you are no longer subconsciously self-sabotaging or self-hating.

An example of this is holding insecurity around your self-worth. On the surface, you feel uncertain about your role in other people's lives, whether you are valued enough or whether you'll ever be desired by the people you care about. When you start to question why you don't feel good enough – when this thought started, where or who it came from and why it came about – you'll find that you had the answer all along.

In this case, let's say you don't feel good enough because people have mistreated you in the past and walked out of your life effortlessly. You don't think you're worthy of love because if you were, people would have loved you more or fought harder to fix the relationship you had. On the surface, you dismissed this limiting belief as a simple lack of confidence, but underneath you have come to doubt and disapprove of yourself as a result of somebody else's actions. You have internalised the belief that you are inferior and it seeps into every aspect of your life. You likely make quick assumptions about the way people feel about you because of this internalised insecurity. You may well project your distorted self-perception onto others, which makes new relationships more difficult. You might even have a habit of going after the wrong people in your life because of your repressed shadow – you feel more comfortable around those who validate the limiting beliefs you have about yourself because deep down you believe true love has to be earned or you must chase or mirror people in order to gain friendship.

The goal of shadow work is to establish a better relationship with your authenticity (which means embracing your insecurities and wounded self) so you do not have an emotional crisis when an unexpected thought or emotion rises to the surface. Shadow work allows you to gain full recognition of every part of yourself so there are no nasty surprises. It will also eliminate the need for a masked self. Masking refers to the practice of hiding your true self to gain wider social acceptance. It involves mirroring other people's behaviours and opinions, rehearsing before speaking to people and making a conscious effort to appear cooler, all because you have an inherent belief that behaving without thought would lead to rejection.

To start with, you can work through the list of shadow work prompts below. When answering these questions, don't pause to analyse or assess the best answer for each one. The point of this exercise is to quickly observe which part of you feels called out to and what immediate response it gives before conscious thought steps in.

- ☐ How are my values different to my family's and how do I feel about those differences?
- ☐ In what ways do I wish to avoid becoming like my family?
- ☐ When do I feel inferior to others? Why?
- ☐ When do I feel superior to others? Why?
- ☐ What do I feel ashamed of? How can I give myself compassion?
- ☐ When was the last time I felt envious of someone? What can this teach me?
- ☐ How would I describe myself? Where can I give myself more credit?
- ☐ How do I treat myself after a mistake? What am I too harsh on myself about?
- ☐ What really bothers me in other people? How can I gain more acceptance around this?

- ☐ What mistake do I need to forgive myself for?
- ☐ If someone was talking behind my back, what would I fear they were talking about the most?
- ☐ How would I reparent my child self?
- ☐ What emotions do I try to avoid feeling?
- ☐ How do I define success and failure in my personal life?
- ☐ What do I try to hide from others? Why?
- ☐ What do I wish others would notice more about me?
- ☐ What is something people often get wrong about me?
- ☐ What expectations do I place on myself? Which feel hard and which feel easy?
- ☐ When do I struggle to trust myself? How can I work on this weakness?
- ☐ What makes me feel valued? How can I give this to myself?
- ☐ What do I most wish I could change about my life up until this point?
- ☐ What are my favourite qualities about myself?
- ☐ When do I feel most grateful?
- ☐ How would I go about your day if I had 100 per cent confidence?
- ☐ What am I proud of myself for? How can I celebrate myself more?
- ☐ What do I need to hear? How can I incorporate this into positive affirmations?

Self-support

An important part of healing is establishing a self-support system. Leaning on your loved ones for advice and support during difficult times can be necessary and helpful, allowing you to feel safer on this journey. But always make sure you are not wholly reliant on other people to offer advice and comfort, which might encourage dependence and prioritises other people's opinions over your own.

The easiest way to build a more loving and trusting bond with yourself is by making emotional regulation a daily habit. Emotional regulation is the psychological process of managing one's own emotions to increase, maintain or lower a certain feeling. This is used to improve wellbeing, relationships and resilience.

Emotional regulation is achieved through 'detachment' and 'attention'. Instead of simply reacting to a situation, you pay attention to where you're feeling the emotion and what's going on around you to detach from the situation and presumably the outburst that could ensue. This allows you to control your emotions, intentionally calm yourself down and observe your reaction rather than succumbing powerlessly to it. Though, importantly, this is not to be confused with controlling what emotions you feel. Part of self-love is accepting yourself even when the ugliest of emotions come to the surface – regulation allows you to control the expression of these emotions.

I used to be overwhelmed with devastation after an argument with my parent. It brought every past issue to the front of my mind and I would sit on my bedroom floor crying my eyes out while facing feelings of low self-worth and shame. I used to internalise these feelings and they became a part of my identity. My confidence took a significant hit and self-doubt clouded my judgement every time I tried to pursue my dreams. But once I made the shift to intentionally process these emotions for my benefit, the battle with myself finally came to a halt. While I allowed myself to feel the full extent of my sadness, anger, fear and shame, instead of picking myself up to carry on as normal, I was able to sit with the emotions and question their presence in a non-judgemental, caring way.

Through observing my emotions from a logical standpoint, validating them and understanding their role in my life, it was easier to see them as an experience rather than a part of my identity. By becoming present with yourself during your most emotional moments, you can start to practise being the kindest person to go to for advice in your life. When you start adopting this role, you'll at least stop being the person criticising yourself and making your self-esteem worse. We can be our biggest enemies. Instead of defining your emotions as a negative part of you – e.g. as anger issues or oversensitivity – you can start to relabel those moments in kinder ways: 'This is just my anxiety being triggered by a tense situation' or 'This is just my anger rising up because I feel a need to be heard and rant it out.'

After this, once you're done processing, you can healthily choose a new feeling. To get you there, you may decide to take a walk, journal, watch a comforting TV show, revisit an old gratitude list, spend quality time with a friend – this is important so as to control the time the emotion gets to receive once you're done feeling it. You don't dwell all week on the fact you cried. You don't feel guilty for the rest of the day for having had an angry outburst. You turn your attention to things you value to instead take control of your day, so your emotions are not allowed to consume you and define you.

At this point in my life, I have a much better hold on my emotions. Whenever I feel like being passive aggressive or having an angry outburst, I've learned to remove myself from the situation temporarily so I don't do anything I regret. I can then process my emotions alone and validate them, question why I might feel that way and pay attention to what I wish the other person would recognise. Then I can go back and communicate those needs to achieve a productive end to what could have been a moment of self-inflicted pain and stress.

Self-compassion

Compassion makes the process of healing much smoother and it is a fundamental pillar to achieving self-love. But before you apply it to yourself, you must give it to others. Everyone is fighting an internal battle you know nothing about – so with this lack of information, why would you assume anything someone says should be taken personally? Choose to move your perception past simply taking someone's actions and words at face value and instead understand what motivates these behaviours.

As we discussed earlier in the section about our shadow selves, people who are unhealed and insecure will be triggered by things around them and so they use their anger and judgement as a way to feel some comfort and normalcy. Happy, secure, grateful people don't have the capacity to act hatefully because they are so focused on the abundance they have created in their own life. When you realise this, all your pain will turn into pity. It will act as a shield, protecting you from the actions of every person you come across. You have to understand that there is a certain level of unfulfilled purpose, energy and unresolved sadness that causes a person to willingly inflict pain onto others. Nothing is ever really about you, so there's no point in attaching to it and internalising it.

Compassion is also paramount in combatting self-sabotaging habits. Self-sabotage is a completely subconscious pattern which is why it's so hard to stop. It is the result of trying to make a drastic change around a situation that previously caused you pain that you suppressed. When similar situations arise in your current life, your nervous system is triggered. Your subconscious thinks you're in danger, which results in sabotaging behaviours as it tries to protect you from the discomfort you experienced with the same situation in the past. Your nervous system seeks out predictability and comfort, anything outside of this can facilitate a self-sabotaging behaviour to reinstate a comfortable and safe feeling. This is what leads us to create our own pain and misery, because if that is what we've had to deal with from a young age, our subconscious will lead us to continuously seek out those environments out of fear of the unknown – even if the unknown is potential happiness and healing.

The only way to combat this is by forcing yourself to explore outside what is known. Changing your behaviour while embracing the inevitable failure and discomfort, getting comfortable with the feeling of danger and reassuring yourself as you go will build up a tolerance that helps you rewire your nervous system to put an end to these self-sabotaging behaviours. This doesn't come easily, so moderation and self-compassion are imperative to making progress on this journey. Plan smaller steps to become self-helping.

For example, instead of dealing with the daunting task of cutting out junk food, try to replace one of your normal sugary snacks a day with a piece of fruit and build up the number of snacks you replace on a weekly basis. If you feel the urge to go back to your temptations, practise self-forgiveness. Just the intention is a huge milestone in your self-love journey and one setback doesn't erase all the progress you've made so far. Remember this isn't a matter of trying to be perfect but instead doing favours for your future self to make their life easier.

Younger self

Your inner child is a part of your subconscious that represents your childhood. It holds all the critical beliefs and teachings that were engrained into our mind from a young age and influenced the way we developed our self-image and what coping mechanisms we use as adults. We hold many painful experiences within this part of us from being shamed, judged, bullied, punished or rejected, which then determine the way we feel about ourselves and how we show up in the world later on in life. Inner child work is the process of reparenting ourselves to shift the narratives of these experiences so we can move on from being stuck at the age of our trauma and instil more positive self-beliefs that allow us to flourish in our adult life.

Writing letters to your younger self is the perfect way to start as it opens up a dialogue with your subconscious mind and gives you the chance to become aware of your younger self's mindset, needs and fears, instead of going through life oblivious to how these things are affecting you. The more you can grasp the inner workings of your childlike mind, the better you can understand how they translate to how your current life looks.

For example, my inner child felt like she never fitted in with anyone else. I then spent years of my life assuming that people didn't like me and that it was hard to make friends. These beliefs that had stuck with me formed a behaviour that created a reality I wasn't happy with. The belief that I was unlikeable influenced my lack of confidence and approach to making friends so much so that I only accepted friendship from those who were brazen in their adoption of me. Consequently, I was surrounded by energy vampires, narcissists and toxic friends because I was too afraid to set boundaries and consciously choose the energy I wanted around me. I was accessible to anybody, which only led to constant friendship drama and break-ups.

Falling more in tune to my younger self and her insecurities allowed me to identify this behaviour and shift it in accordance with the belief I wanted to have – that I could have aligned friendships, I was charming to others and I could talk to anybody I desired. Understanding the gap between my belief system and my desires encouraged me to embody the traits of the person I wanted to be and act on that, no matter how uncomfortable it seemed. After consistent practice, I finally had enough evidence to invalidate my inner child's feelings of social awkwardness and rejection.

When using letter-writing as a form of inner child work

you could place yourself back in the shoes of your six-, seven- or eight-year-old self and write a letter to your current self, explaining that time in your life, what you need and what you wish for. Write a letter in response to that letter, taking on the role of your own parent validating your inner child's concerns and feelings. Reparenting yourself in this way heals the gaps in the care you actually received as a child and can start to build up the self-love and self-worth that was originally affected by those supressed and unsupported emotions.

The simplest way to build up self-love through inner child work is simply considering the inner child on a daily basis. We often hold ourselves to such high standards and harsh judgements, we forget to be gentle with ourselves. Keeping a picture of your younger self by your mirror, on your phone wallpaper or in your wallet reminds you of the treatment you truly deserve and how important the dreams of that little girl are and how much fight and self-compassion you need to commit to making those dreams come true every day.

Identity shifting

Lastly, let's talk about the importance of shifting your identity. The goal of this is to positively change your self-concept. It starts with releasing the limited perceptions you may have of the world and yourself. You can't keep holding onto the patterns that have gotten you to a place you're unsatisfied with. You can make all the habitual changes you wish, but if your self-concept looks the same, you will always struggle to become the ideal version of yourself.

According to Sigmund Freud, 'age regression' is the result of failing to emotionally progress past the age you experienced your trauma. This is the ego's way of protecting itself from emotionally intense and negative experiences. Thus, your emotional maturity will be stuck at that point in time because you have not processed those feelings or developed your inner belief system.

A lot of the time we have physically moved into different environments and phases of our lives, but our progression is compromised because we still identify as the previous version of ourselves. You need to update your self-concept regularly by aligning it to who you wish to become rather than holding on to who you think you always will be. There's a misconception that this is a form of 'being fake' and losing your authenticity, but I would argue that this is the most authentic act of all – you are finally letting go of your years of conditioning from others and the coping mechanisms you've developed in survival mode to finally take a step back to decide who you want to be and then creating that.

Identity shifting is done through implementing habits that you imagine your ideal self would have. Self-love is the discipline that encourages you to take that action now because your ideal self can only live in that way if your current self starts today. Not only do you need to change your habits, but also the way you see yourself so that you can remain consistent in practising those habits. For example, you're not just going to try to start a business – you *are* a business owner. You're not just facing your fears with exposure therapy – you *are* a confident person. You don't need to abandon your previous self-concept but rather update it so that you can keep growing without harbouring the thoughts that weigh you down.

Your ideal self isn't one without flaws (that's impossible), it's the self that tries its best. The goal of focusing on improvement isn't perfection or changing who you are on the whole, but having the self-awareness to work on the things that hold you back from being the person you were always supposed to be, if insecurities, trauma and ego hadn't got in the way. It's about loving yourself enough to resist your brain's chase for dopamine in order to prioritise what will do you good overall, even though it might feel painful in the present moment. It can be as small as swapping the comfort of your bed for a morning workout, which would improve your mental health, fitness and energy, therefore elevating the life you experience daily. But this is not just limited to routines, it shows when you resist the urge to talk to the guy who makes you feel great because you've improved your self-love enough to see he falls short of your high standards. How you do anything is how you do everything.

Your self-image is at the centre of your ability to be confident in loving yourself, but as we go through life, we experience heartbreak, betrayal and rejection – all of which can harm our self-image. The only true way to create a new, positive self-image is by creating a new normal. Using the healing methods described in this chapter is imperative to processing the emotions so they don't come up as triggers in unexpected moments, but after that you have to decide who you are without the baggage.

Your self-love is developed in the micro moments of your life – the first thing you do when you wake up every morning, the way you speak to yourself, how you show up in the world and allow yourself to be seen, how big you dream, how you feel when you think about your goals and everything in between. Self-improvement is about creating a version of yourself you are *excited* to be.

Who would you be if this was the first day of your life? If you woke up with all the knowledge and wisdom you possess but without memory of what happened in the past? I'm sure you would carry yourself fearlessly and talk to yourself more kindly. By looking to the future and who you want to become, the intensity of the shame you hold around your past reduces with every day you make that image of your potential clearer. This starts with implementing new routines and habits which help shift your thought patterns. When you wake up and go about your life differently, it signals separation and cuts the cord between your two lives – the wounded past and the healed present. Your identity is formed of your values, actions and where you spend your time. It can be something as small as changing the way you dress, which makes you feel like a brand new person and allows you to practise new thought patterns more confidently.

CHAPTER SUMMARY

- [ ] You do not need to isolate yourself to heal. Putting yourself in social environments before you feel ready can help move you along the healing process. You'll be exposed to your previous triggers and challenging situations, providing opportunities to implement your new mindset and coping mechanisms to ensure they stick with you at all times.
- [ ] Healing has no timeline or destination. It is lifelong and inevitably paired with negative emotions. Trying to rid yourself of these will only prolong the journey as you continue to reject very normal parts of yourself.
- [ ] This journey isn't about becoming somebody new, it's about coming home to the version of yourself you were always supposed to be, but without the insecurities that were added along the way. Fall in love with the parts of your life that set you apart from everybody else. Maybe your life wasn't meant to look like anyone else's; maybe this pain was necessary and a part of what will make you better than ever.
- [ ] Don't go back to what doesn't serve you. Stop fetishising your sadness and create a self-concept and lifestyle that distances you from painful memories so that you can put your happiness first without being reminded of everything in the past.
- [ ] Shadow work is a crucial part of healing. It involves exploring and questioning your limiting beliefs until you get to the root cause of them so that you can finally replace them with positive affirmations that benefit your life.

CHAPTER HOMEWORK

- ☐ There is no such thing as being perfectly healed. Put yourself in an environment or situation in which you think you will struggle to practise putting the healing you've completed thus far to use. It could be public speaking, going on a first date or just allowing yourself to be seen in your authenticity.
- ☐ Honour your negative feelings – journal, rant, start a video diary, vent to a friend, cry and or scream for an entire day if you wish. Don't hold onto the emotion, express it so you can finally let it go.
- ☐ Spend an hour looking back at childhood photos or videos and think about how they were feeling and how they imaged your life would look now. Write a letter to them or simply keep their presence in your mind. You are living for your younger self too – let this boost the compassion you give to yourself.
- ☐ Create new narratives from the experiences that bother you most. Start meeting people where they're at and give them compassion as you imagine their experience and capacity to be kind. People cannot be kind to you because they are not kind to themselves. This is not to excuse their behaviour but instead to grant yourself peace and protect your self-worth from crumbling at the treatment you receive from unhealed people.

CHAPTER 6:

TRANSFORMING A BREAK-UP

How do I get over somebody?

Most of us feel that break-ups are a failure. *You picked wrong! How could you not see the signs? Now you have to start all over. I can't believe you wasted so much time. If he couldn't love you, who else would?* Wrong.

Really, break-ups are an inevitable step towards finding the most compatible person for us. We are not born with all the information on what we need, what would make us happy and what life we should build for ourselves – because that's what the journey of life is for! Every trial and tribulation offers a new clue you can use in building the jigsaw that is your life. Every break-up teaches you exactly what doesn't work, despite your previous assumption that it might have. It gives you new insight into what you'll look for next time and improves your list of non-negotiable standards. The more break-ups you embrace, the better and more detailed your knowledge of the right person for you.

We tend to fear the break-up when we fear our lack of possibilities outside the relationship. I clung to unsuitable partners because I felt 'lucky' to even 'get them' in the first place. But imagine if someone guaranteed your soulmate is on their way to you, craving your energy and everything that makes you, you. They are everything you loved about your previous partners combined and without any of the incompatibilities. They just adore you, showering you in romance daily and finally showing you the kind of lifestyle your younger self could only have dreamed of. You get everything you want.

Just imagine hearing that. Well, guess what . . . YOU are the person who's supposed to be offering that reassurance. If you were thinking that scenario sounds unrealistic, it's a sign that you need to work on your belief system. Realism is just pessimism repackaged. Why are you setting limits on yourself and determining what realistic looks like for you when you haven't even been down that path yet? Why don't you believe that you're worthy of the fairy-tale romance you once desired? Why do you assume this is not easy? Is it because you're generalising every relationship based on the several bad dating experiences you've had? Is it because you focus more on the idea of changing them instead of moving on and saving your time? Or is it because you're constantly digesting stories of dating fails, cheating betrayals and celebrity cheating scandals?

Self-loving favours

We don't get our desired results when dating because we're not ready for them. This is entirely different to being worthy of them.

You feel badly when comparing your dating life to the progress others are making, assuming they have something you don't. But the only difference between a person with a flourishing love life and one who is stuck in their singlehood is resistance. Resistance comes in the form of your attachment style, confidence, self-image, mindset, life experience and habits. Your singlehood is not a sign of your unpleasantness, it is simply a resource that prepares you for the relationship you need. It does not mean there are no good men around, it means that you are blind to their presence because you have not aligned to the version of yourself that matches their energy. A person who fails to see the blessings in a life alone will only ever be capable of accepting the wrong relationships. You do not crave partnership, you crave connection and because you have not given it to yourself, you search for it in all the wrong places in pursuit of immediate gratification from another person.

A romantic partner cannot save you or provide happiness, they are simply the addition to an already fulfilling life that you have created on your own terms. The intellectual stimulation you crave can be found in the books you read; the adventure you dream of can be experienced on the dates you take yourself on; the companionship you wish for will come from networking with people who start inspiring conversations. Everything you seek from a relationship is possible to find in your solitude. Your purpose is so much greater than just being someone's partner. If you feel yourself crumbling from the way a person left, shift your attention away from the ending and feel reassurance in the fact that love had to be felt for it to have the power to break you. Let yourself fall apart, without the need to close off your heart; it will heal and adapt among dozens of separations throughout your life. In a world where so many people play it safe with their feelings, find comfort in the fact that you experienced complexity and completeness.

Love doesn't have to last forever to make it a significant story. Some relationships and people come into our lives to allow us to see the voids we've been oblivious to, even when we mistakenly try to fill them with their presence. The entire point of this journey was to lead you back to healing through your temporary timeline together. You want to walk into the life you deserve as the person you are supposed to be, and the people we meet and lose along the way help us to fulfil that. Adjusting to a life without them won't be easy; you will lose them over and over again with every familiar song, street, sight or story that sends you into a nostalgic reminiscence. You won't forget someone overnight; you will lose yourself in every alternative ending and feel their absence as you start a life alone after knowing what it felt to live by their side. In the face of this struggle, stay stubborn in your truth, because not everyone is worthy of the joy that is you. Realise that you are an experience that is reserved for the mutual love that protects you and doesn't play with you. Know when to let something go so that you can finally find the love within yourself. And then, slowly, as you return to be the centre of your own universe, you will realise you are creating happiness without the one you thought you couldn't be happy without.

Break-up to-do list

The actions in this list helped me in creating a happy life after heartbreak. They healed the wound rather than providing 'quick fixes' that simply protected my ego and neglected the pain at hand.

- [ ] Experience every emotion to its full extent until you are done with it.
- [ ] Silence the lies nostalgia tells you (delete photos, block their phone number, throw away their belongings).
- [ ] Seek comfort with friends and family to remind yourself of the love that still exists.
- [ ] Write a list of the reasons you shouldn't be together – it will be your safety net for the days heartache takes over.
- [ ] Create new excitement in your life (plan a weekend away, join a class, try new food).
- [ ] Let go of who you once were and build who you will grow to be (action the things you were too busy to do).
- [ ] Create a new routine and life – don't live a life they were associated with.
- [ ] Work on the traits that allowed you to tolerate the wrong person for so long. Let this become a habit which ensures every relationship is always an improvement from the last one because of the self-awareness and work that takes place in between (attachment style, co-dependency, emotional availability, self-validation).
- [ ] Go back to a place that once represented your lost love and change the narrative of it (solo date there).

SITUATIONSHIPS

A situationship brings the benefits of a relationship without any of the labels. It's a way to gain complete romantic access to someone without any of the commitment. So, when it all comes crumbling down, can you be heartbroken over someone who was never really yours? The answer is yes. After all, situationships involve attachment and connection; it's the loyalty and green flags they lack. Yet so many decide to stay. Why?

Most likely you let your heart guide you instead of your mind, which has entrapped you in a situation that doesn't exist. You let your feelings cloud your judgement to give you false hope of a reality that isn't possible. You weren't observing what was happening in the moment because you were daydreaming of a future with a person who kept hurting you in the present. You run from communication, just to get swept up with meaningless gestures that fulfil your delusions. You exclaim that you know you deserve better and yet you stay, day after day – maybe even year after year.

Is this the person who deserves you in your absoluteness with all the love, compassion and care you offer? Is this the best you've ever experienced? Perhaps you believe you can't help how you feel. In your view at the time, you get them, you love them, you have a connection unmatched and you say 'it's rare'. No. What's rare is deciding to stay with someone who hurts you and then going back for seconds. What's rare is questioning your worth over a person you claim to care so much about. What's rare is giving up the opportunity of a better life to stay with the person who refuses to give you any more.

You give so much compassion to their negligence and never enough to the suffering you are dealt. You believe more in their empty promises and mismatched actions than the love you're really worthy of. Love isn't hard and doesn't involve proving your worth, because the right person will make the time to understand you and you them. People can only meet you as far as they've met themselves. If they choose not to make an effort, this is not a measure of your value but rather the depth of the connection they have with themselves. You cannot expect someone who doesn't accept their own emotions to be in tune with yours. You cannot wait for someone who doesn't give themselves kindness to shower you in it. You cannot keep waiting for someone to do the inner work that will make this bond straightforward if they keep refusing to do it.

FRIENDS

You cannot lose a person that was never yours. So often, we love to label people as our forever and place them within a future before they earned a place there. We worry about the timelines of our unions with others in an attempt to avoid endings and heartache at all costs. But endings are a sign of growth and redirection.

Outgrowing friends should be a moment of peace, not guilt. No one is entitled to more time than you are willing to offer. There is power in knowing when to let go. When you sit among the people who used to light you up just to find yourself feeling lonely in their company and drained after every interaction, it's a sign of your expansion. You are flourishing into a human who is so much bigger than their childhood group of friends; there are so many parts of you that are pushing you to reach bigger heights in unfamiliar places. So, when you realise that you wouldn't be friends with the people you met before you knew yourself if you met them as your current self, it is time for you to move on. Be confident enough to honour this feeling rather than forcing yourself to stay with those with whom you lack connection, out of fear of their reaction. It is not rude or selfish to acknowledge your growth and direct your attention elsewhere for your own wellbeing. You do not owe anyone more parts of yourself than you have already given. If you feel guilty for the pain you might inflict in doing what's right for you, remember it is not your responsibility to carry the burden of other people's reactions to the point where it prevents you from honouring your needs.

Losing a friendship and feeling uncertain as to why is not a reason to concern yourself with every possible explanation to the point where you are left questioning all that is good about you. Relinquish the need to blame yourself and have trust in your path.

More often than not, broken bonds are due to falling out of frequency with one another. When you cannot explain why you no longer talk or why things don't feel the way they used to, it is because the frequency you are vibrating at no longer aligns with the frequency of that friendship. You are no longer a match for each other because your growth has taken you down a different path.

Friendship loss can be an opportunity, but you will fail to see it if your ego is running your life. This will lead you to take people's actions personally, blame the world for being unfair or start to hate yourself for having 'failed yet again'. If you allow this loss to define you, it will rob you of your confidence. You are not how many friends you have, nor are you how many have left you. You are what you do with those experiences. If we feel unlucky to have fewer friends, it's often because we are defining ourselves by quantity over quality – it sounds cliché but self-love is about what energies you tolerate and allow access to your life. People who concern themselves with popularity find themselves at the mercy of validation from others. They therefore find themselves stuck in groups full of gossip, mistrust and misalignment. It is the best example of having poor spiritual hygiene. You will adopt the energies you surround yourself with and become the average of the mindsets you converse with. Pay attention to the way you wish to feel and get picky around the people you give your time to – their influence has the power to build or knock your self-image so remember this the next time you tolerate disrespect out of your fear of 'losing people'.

Romantic relationships, situationships and friendships are all susceptible to painful break-ups, but a common solution in easing the pain is the law of detachment . . .

DETACHMENT

'Why don't you have a relationship with your dad?'

'If I was different, he wouldn't have left.'

This is 'attachment' and your self-love will always suffer because of it. Attachment is a strong emotional bond to another person and one way to understand this stems from attachment theory, which was developed by psychologists Joel Bowlby and Mary Ainsworth. You are attached to the idea of someone, their presence in your life and the need to please them, even if it means betraying yourself in the moment. Everyone's actions are completely concerned with their own lives, their triggers and their wounded selves. Being on the receiving end of someone's poor behaviour does not make it your fault or about your imperfections.

A common misconception is that detachment involves the absence of emotion and care. This is untrue. Detachment is simply the process of letting people be and not taking their actions or opinions personally. Detachment is the loss of all expectation. You live fully in the present without questioning whether someone will fall apart or hurt in the future. You are simply living in the experience as it is happening without attaching yourself to its outcomes.

Detachment is an important lesson that should stay with you long beyond your healing phase and it will truly change your life for the better. Letting go and releasing the need to take things personally comes when you understand the following:

- Other people perceive you in a way that suits them. People put you in a box according to the information and biases they hold about the world. They compare you to the life they've experienced and judge you accordingly. No one can view you truly in an unbiased way.
- Nothing is ever personal. People are complex and dealing with a dozen things that you know nothing

about. You have no idea of their demons, insecurities and limiting beliefs that encourage them to act in the way they do. People are only ever trying to act in their own best interests – it's got nothing to do with intentionally hurting you.

- Not every experience is meant to last forever. We are simply limited episodes in the multi-season stories of each other's lives.
- Don't force things. It is when you finally surrender control of external situations that you can release attachment from your life. Focus on grasping every opportunity from your present moment and working on what is within your control instead – e.g. yourself, your feelings, your reactions and your actions.
- Uncertainty is a part of life and a gift. Turn it into a moment of gratitude rather than resentment. Instead of being concerned about the unpredictable actions of others, focus on the fact that every day is a mystery and holds the possibility of being the best day of your life. Allow yourself to be surprised by life.
- Let people be. It will show you their true intentions faster and make your life easier in the long run. Don't try to control what you can't – it causes unnecessary pain and people will always behave in the way they intend to. Your interference simply prolongs the process.
- Life will unfold how it is meant to. Life is not personally attacking you. Adversity is a gift, not a curse. Instead of stressing about how and when

things will come, trust in your path and that you will inevitably attain your desires.

These laws of detachment are liberating. Remembering these basic mindset shifts will free you from unnecessary hurt over the actions of others ever again.

HOW TO GO ABOUT A BREAK-UP

There are two different ways to go about a break-up. The 'regular' way is familiar, it comforts our ego, grows our victim complex, vilifies the other person and fosters unhealthy coping mechanisms to move past our difficulty with this 'rejection'. But I think there's a much better way to deal with heartbreak and it's by moving on from a place of self-love. This type of break-up healing focuses on what's in your control and so you are the centre of attention (instead of obsessing over another person). It means using this pain for growth and wisdom to forge a better path to new and improved experiences.

Regular break-up	Self-love break-up
'It's not fair, why couldn't they fight harder for our relationship?'	Other people's actions have nothing to do with you. They simply acted based on their capabilities. It could be down to their attachment style. It does not signify what you're worthy of.

TRANSFORMING A BREAK-UP

Regular break-up	Self-love break-up
'What if they move on and find happiness with someone new?'	What someone does after the break-up does not represent how they feel about you. Someone will jump into another relationship to avoid dealing with the heartache. Regardless, it is none of your business. Your happiness comes first and if they couldn't elevate it, you should make peace with the fact they'll won't be taking up any more of your time.
'What if I never find that deep connection with someone again?'	What if you find the person you always deserved? Someone who meets every one of your standards with ease. Why wouldn't you do the favour of thinking that way for yourself?
'I invested so much time and energy just for it to be wasted.'	Love is never a waste; it is a lesson.
'Maybe I should reach out. What if they miss me too? I want to get back together.'	To go back to what broke you is to disrespect yourself. Even if it ended on good terms, there is no reason to voluntarily put your energy in a place it no longer aligns to. This can mean sacrificing all that is truly meant for you.

CHAPTER SUMMARY

- ☐ Break-ups are a tool in finding the life we deserve and understanding the details of what we desire from ourselves and others. With every single one comes more clarity and wisdom in who you are and how you need to grow because people come into our lives for a reason – to teach us about ourselves.
- ☐ Running away from the grief of losing someone only keeps you in that place of pain for longer. Allow yourself to break until you are done with it. Feeling the sadness to its full extent is just as important as the moving on stage afterwards. Don't judge yourself for how you feel or how significant the relationship should have been to you. Healing is about accepting how you are instead of chasing how you *should be*.
- ☐ You cannot lose a person who was never yours. People are only experiences given to us for the necessary timeline we were supposed to have them. Be grateful for the lessons without desiring forever from someone who was never supposed to give you it.
- ☐ Losing people is a normal part of life. It signifies your growth and evolution as a person. Not everyone will align with you for the rest of your life. It doesn't make either of you bad people, it's simply two people following the paths they are meant for.
- ☐ Detachment is the art of letting go and releasing the need to take things personally. You release control of things and people, embrace uncertainty and allow life to happen

as it will without stressing over outcomes. You immerse yourself in the present.

CHAPTER HOMEWORK

- ☐ Journal about the gratitude you have for the period of time you had with that person. This allows you to shift into a mentality of loving people for who they are rather how long you need them to be in your life. It also builds the habit of accepting the life you've been given and trusting in your journey.
- ☐ Look out for your future self so you don't continue to accept low-standard behaviour. Use your feelings, as they are fresh, to write a list detailing every reminder of why that person should not be in your life. One day, nostalgia will take over and that list will protect you from going back to a life that is undeserving of you.
- ☐ Remove their access to your life. Even if you don't talk anymore, you don't need their energy lingering or reminders of them in the new life you are creating. Prioritise your future over their temporary feelings. They will move on.
- ☐ Do something cringe. In the discomfort of it, allow yourself to see that you cannot control what others think of you. Detach from how you are going to be seen so that you can finally focus on what you have always wanted to do.
- ☐ Refer back to the break-up to-do list on page 171 any time you need to.

CHAPTER 7:

SPENDING A YEAR ALONE

How can you be alone but not lonely?

It was a cold night in December and I had arrived back home at midnight from an evening with my best friend. We'd been to a drive-in movie theatre together because my recent break-up had left me with a spare ticket. Despite my protests, my friend had decided it would be a good idea to go and get my mind off my ex. It didn't work of course; I had spent the last week thinking uncontrollably about him – how he was feeling, if he was in as much pain as me, if he would finally change or if he had already moved on. Even after I'd admitted the stress he put me through and the chasing I'd had to do just to feel somewhat desired in our relationship, I was still so consumed by him. So naturally, as soon as I got home, I opened Instagram to search his name, wrongfully thinking it would console my broken heart.

After a few seconds of scrolling, I discovered he had followed several girls, including his ex, on social media. I was immediately filled with an overload of conflicting emotions. I was angry at him but disappointed in myself for ignoring the signs. I felt insecure and also a need to find out more to get closure. But most of all, I was fed up. I had spent the last three years of my life healing from heartbreaks to prepare myself for my next 'true love', but when was I ever going to heal the part of me that tolerated these experiences to prepare myself for a life filled with happiness, success and growth? New Year's Eve was just around the corner and, as my devastation slowly started to turn into rage, I looked deep into my reflection in the mirror and made a promise to myself – to spend an entire year alone.

The purpose of this was to salvage the last pieces of the self-respect I had left. If I could successfully go a full year without dating or involving myself in anything that could lead to romance, then I could finally take back control of my life. In the meantime, I decided my days and mind would only be filled with building my career, investing in my friendships and doing something every day that helped me grow into the kind of woman I would be proud of. Men would be completely off limits.

The first week of the New Year felt amazing. Physically, I felt a shift in energy. I woke up happier every day because I finally had a purpose that put me at the centre of my own life for once and my motivation to prove my limiting beliefs wrong was at an all-time high. I would spend the start of every day working out and meditating as a part of the rigorous new morning routine I had set myself. My spare time was taken up with classes or learning new skills online to distance myself from my old identity and I found euphoria in the focus I was putting into my friendships.

However, it wasn't long before I discovered my elation was

only a temporary result of the sense of adventure this new mindset brought about.

Eventually, the inspiring hobbies and meticulous routines felt like every other day and the loneliness started to kick in. My mind would run away to romanticise the days of being somebody's – being bought flowers and taken on dates, knowing I always had a person to talk to at the end of a stressful day. I had experienced this longing before and it always led me right back to where I had started. So, I quit doing what I knew, because that's what had got me here in the first place, and I decided to look at it differently. Relationships brought a kind of love into my life I wasn't getting from anyone else, so what if I figured out a way to give it to myself? This completely changed the trajectory from a bet to go without dating to a year of loving myself unconditionally, and it all started with the idea of taking myself on a date . . .

SOLO DATE BUCKET LIST

- ☐ Take yourself out to dinner
- ☐ Sit in a cosy café and drink your favourite latte
- ☐ Find a nearby lake/pond/ocean to sit by and read your book under the sun
- ☐ Try something new by yourself – pilates, yoga, painting class, book club, running
- ☐ Wake up earlier to watch the sunrise
- ☐ Go to a concert
- ☐ Take yourself on a picnic
- ☐ See theatre

- ☐ Make a candlelit dinner for one at home
- ☐ Be a tourist in your own city
- ☐ Go to a poetry slam
- ☐ Try fruit picking
- ☐ Visit a museum or art gallery
- ☐ Take yourself for a spa day or weekend
- ☐ Have a self-care night at home
- ☐ Book a facial
- ☐ Get a massage
- ☐ Explore a nearby city for the day
- ☐ Paint at home
- ☐ Do some vision boarding / mood board creation
- ☐ Set up a photoshoot for yourself to honour and mark your beauty
- ☐ Go for a night out in a jazz bar
- ☐ Go hiking
- ☐ Build a cosy blanket fort to watch movies from all day
- ☐ Take a scenic bike ride or walk
- ☐ Go stargazing
- ☐ See a film
- ☐ Go to a wildlife sanctuary
- ☐ Have a day at the beach
- ☐ Visit an aquarium
- ☐ Go ice skating
- ☐ Have a late-night dessert date
- ☐ Do some baking
- ☐ Have a day of themed eating – e.g. based around a cuisine, colour or movie
- ☐ Try a mindfulness colouring book

- ☐ Go to a comedy show
- ☐ Create a memory scrapbook
- ☐ Take a digital detox challenge – 24 hours without your phone, tablet or TV!
- ☐ Do some gardening
- ☐ Start a DIY project
- ☐ Write letters to your future self
- ☐ Get on a flight and travel!
- ☐ Buy yourself flowers

While some of these may differ from traditional dates, it boils down to committing to spending quality time with yourself to grow your self-love consistently.

Tam's top tips

After years of solo dating and teaching my online audience how to do so, I have learned what truly makes solo dates 'productive' in establishing self-love versus just spending some time alone and I've broken this down into the following checklist to make it easy to remember:

- ☐ Step outside of your comfort zone. The most loving thing you can do for yourself is to expose yourself to unfamiliar environments so your confidence can flourish long term. You will sacrifice your short-term comforts and feelings for the benefit of your future self through exposure therapy (the act of exposing yourself to the things you usually avoid until you feel numb to the fear you used to feel).

- ☐ Have confidence. Similarly, self-love is elevating your needs to such a high level of importance that the thought of other people's judgement wouldn't even cross your mind. And why would they? Why would a stranger's (assumed) negative opinion be more significant than your freedom to do something alone and love every second of it? Self-love is also letting go of your fear of being perceived. Allow yourself to take up space, be seen and be heard – you should know you deserve it. Plus, why does the thought of being perceived automatically equate to judgement in your mind? What if someone's admiring you? What if they love your outfit or can't keep their eyes off your confident aura? You think you are being judged because you are judging yourself. The more solo date experiences you conquer, the quicker you'll realise no one was obsessing over you in the first place.
- ☐ Start small. Protect your self-esteem at all costs during this process as it will be the key to your consistency. Don't feel pressure to do everything alone all at once when you're only at the beginning of your journey. It is normal to feel uncomfortable or unsure about enjoying time alone in this phase, so be gentle with yourself. I found café dates the easiest and I did those weekly for three months before I mustered up the courage to go to restaurants. When that felt like a breeze to me, I stepped it up and went to a concert alone. After two whole years of solo dating, I finally got around to travelling to another country by myself. Everyone has a different pace so set yourself mini goals. Going to the cinema is easy because you're sat in the

dark and entertained! At home solo dates are even simpler. Your first goal can be to commit one day of the week or month to a consistent solo date. Afterwards, you can start working your way through the solo date bucket list in a way that suits you but still prioritises new environments and exposure therapy.

- ☐ No devices. Sitting in a restaurant alone waiting for your food to arrive while surrounded by tables filled with groups and couples can feel awkward, so you naturally grab your phone to keep your hands and gaze busy and to take your attention away from the fear or boredom you might feel otherwise. But would you be scrolling on your phone for 30 minutes during a date with somebody else? The point of solo dating is to give yourself even more of the effort, energy and treatment that you pour out for everyone else. Using your phone or watching Netflix is simply a distraction from genuinely spending quality time with yourself. You are yet again avoiding the process of being alone with your thoughts and all the learnings that come from this and experiencing the world by yourself. Unplug, you'll get more out of it.
- ☐ Dress up. Put effort into your appearance just like you would for another. You carry yourself with higher vibrations when you feel good about the way you've presented yourself. Spending time alone isn't an excuse to be lazy because 'no one will see me anyway'; it provides even more reason to go all out, to make a point out of the fact that you are the only person you'll ever need to impress.

- ☐ Make it a commitment. Solo dating isn't simply an idea or a to-do list task that gets pushed back with every new activity that comes along. You will not postpone it for friends, you won't readjust it to make it to that party – you will show up to the reservations that you made or with the tickets that you bought in advance because you would never cancel on yourself. Schedule your solo dates in your calendar and create resistance that ensures they become an uncancellable plan, such as reservations, tickets, strict timings.
- ☐ Plan an itinerary. Likewise, planning your date days in advance is crucial to be able to make presence, gratitude and enjoyment the focus. So, you should plan out transport, locations and timings in advance to avoid stress on the day. This also helps build up excitement and allows you to put in extra prior thought to ensure you're giving yourself the best experience possible. I will always research a few different restaurants and activities before I pick my favourite combination. I also prefer to plan for these in the daytime, in busy public locations because it makes me feel safer.
- ☐ Document the experience. Take pictures and videos of every new experience you embark on. After a year of solo dating, you will be more than grateful that you can physically see the journey you went on and the growth that every photo represents. I look back on photos from my solo dates and it transports me in time, as I remember exactly how I was feeling at that moment, the pride I had in myself when I completed it and the unique experience

that every single one brought, like meeting new people, trying new foods or improving my confidence. It helps in romanticising your life and holds you accountable in making this a consistent practice. You could start a video diary or challenge yourself to compete the solo date bucket list in one year and compile a slideshow or scrapbook from your pictured year of self-love.

- [ ] It's important to remember to always tell someone where you are going, keep your phone charged, share your location with a friend and try to travel in the day as much as you can.

LOVING YOURSELF

Love is a behaviour not a feeling. Don't concern yourself with what's it supposed to be like or how you should be feeling. Your only consideration should be how you show up for yourself every day and with what intention. Self-love is the consistent act of care and effort for yourself, regardless of your circumstances and mistakes – just how you'd express love for another person. You wouldn't expect somebody else to be free of all flaws and have their life in perfect order to be worthy of love and effort, so why would you place that standard upon yourself?

A lot of the time, we claim to love ourselves because it feels like the natural thing to say. 'Well, it's me! *Obviously*, I love myself; it's not like I hate myself!' Except it's not so obvious and it's not a matter of love versus hate. When you look at the intention behind most people's 'acts of love' it's often very conditional and illustrates an active attempt to gain something to feel better about themselves or avoid what they dislike about themselves. It's common to feel that you're showing up for yourself through actioning a certain task or achieving goals, but this behaviour is motivated by academic validation, a need to impress others or chasing the idea of who you should be rather than accepting who you are now without any accolades or admiration.

Take a highly successful businessperson, for example. They could naturally assume they're full of self-love because they feel confident in themselves, but their behaviour and intention may contradict this if they deprive themselves of sleep, miss out on social time to get more work done or neglect self-care to focus on making more money. Their desire for wealth may be driven by superiority and status, meaning they always chase the next best thing. If their health and wellbeing seem like a chore, they dismiss self-reflection to avoid any 'unnecessary' negative emotions and focus more on performing as someone they believe would be worthy of respect and recognition, then they are not honouring their authenticity. Loving yourself values unconditional acceptance – this is a valid intention behind the act of doing what's in your best interest paired with a repeated set of loving behaviours, like setting boundaries and taking breaks.

A highly successful businessperson actively practising self-love lives differently. They focus on their work and goals while setting non-negotiable boundaries for rest time and they schedule time to reflect, journal or solo date. They have a healthy routine in place to take care of their mental health, including exercising, eating well, social time and gratitude, and they go to therapy to balance the attention they give to their output and input. They understand their needs and alter their lifestyle according to that – not the other way around.

Having said this, though, love is a series of choices and it's not as clear-cut as having a healthy routine and taking time out to rest – it will change alongside the events of your personal life and the emotions you may be dealing with. For example, when I was putting a lot of work into my career and self-growth, I hit a wall every evening where I was overwhelmed by self-doubt. I had struggled with this feeling for several years and continued to dismiss it, thinking it wasn't a big deal (an act of self-avoidance rather than self-love). I realised I was behaving as if I was too difficult to deal with and so I took the time to get to the root of the feeling through a new set of behaviours: I practised shadow work journaling, inner child work and worked on my inner dialogue. This was a temporary routine which served me at the time and helped me to transform my self-doubt into self-confidence. Loving yourself can be difficult and require constant change – but that's the essence of it: you sit with the discomfort and inconvenience of pressing pause on all the things you're supposed to be doing in life to take time to care for yourself.

So how do we love ourselves unconditionally? It's not setting a limit on how long you can feel an emotion, not putting pressure on having to be A-okay, not limiting the time you need to rest, not beating yourself up for not looking or acting a certain way – ultimately, it's understanding you deserve love on your worst day. Your skin can be broken out, you could have skipped the gym for a month and lost a job – but you still deserve kindness, good energy and care. Of course, you will still take action to change your circumstances – like moving your body to benefit your mental health – but on the days you fail, the kindness remains. We focus so much on trying to love others unconditionally and yet we deny ourselves of this limitless acceptance. It should be the opposite. Love to others should always be conditional: that in itself is self-love.

People have no problem giving chance after chance to the partner that doesn't show up for them, or they stay in friendships full of judgement, or they keep giving access and resources to toxic family members . . . so why is it that when *you* make a mistake, you can't stand yourself? Your mind can fill with every possible insult, every new insecurity, every ounce of shame, every reason as to why you're not worthy or deserving of the love you dream of, yet you may give it out so abundantly to those who don't deserve it. It is far more important to give yourself grace in your moments of low confidence than to give all the comfort in the world to the friend who continues to drain your energy with their endless problems and victim mentality.

Setting conditions for your relationships with others isn't selfish, it's self-respecting. Why would you give love and time to someone who doesn't align with you? Someone else's need to be loved and cared for is not your responsibility. It is not your job to fix and heal everyone – only yourself. Your relationships with others are reserved for reciprocated effort and love with people who meet the standards you have set for your life: they don't gossip, they celebrate your wins, your conversations leave you energised and they support you. The absence of these qualities absolutely requires a re-evaluation of the bond and whether it is good for you. That is not to say you abandon them in their times of need or when they make mistakes, but rather assess their role in your life on a normal day and question whether it meets your expectation of a healthy friendship.

True love is only possible with conditions, otherwise it is used as a weapon to step all over you and get away with it in the name of 'love'. Conditions are the necessary behaviours that are needed to be able to love someone fully. Unconditional love values feeling over action, which is merely attachment and infatuation. The real process of love is consistently showing effort which is in accordance with the other person's needs. Unconditional love is important in the relationship to yourself because it is the only bond you will have to reside in for the rest of your life.

Self-love should not be assumed because it never comes naturally. We are raised by our parents' preferences, we are controlled in education, we are given insecurities from the media, we are pressured to fit in by our peers, we are conditioned to find romantic love in a certain timescale. How would we ever automatically know how to love ourselves when our entire lives have been centred around everyone but ourselves? On top of that, how are we to truly know who we are when we spend every day performing for every standard society expects us to meet? If we move like machines, constantly just trying to get through the day, pass an exam, make more money, have more friends, achieve a certain lifestyle and try to become happy at some point then of course we won't love ourselves because when have we ever had time to get to know ourselves away from the eyes of others?

We think we know ourselves, but often we only know the form we take on in different environments: the way we behave at home to keep the peace, the way we perform at a party to make others laugh, the way we hide ourselves away from judgement in the workplace. We are constantly aware of the way we're being perceived and reacted to, always considering how we can influence the people around us. A year alone gives you the attention to learn how to love the truest version of you.

HOW TO SPEND IT

This isn't just about solo dating, that's just the tip of the iceberg. There is a range of different self-loving behaviours you can use to make the most from your year alone. It all starts with your intention:

INTENTION	SELF-LOVING ACTS
Focus on building my dream life and self.	Planning my week ahead in accordance with my yearly goals and scheduling them in time blocks to stay efficient and manage my self-care time too. Vision boarding the life I desire and using this to visualise and form my affirmative inner dialogue at the start of every morning. Acting in a way that aligns to the future version of myself. E.g. swapping complaining for gratitude.

INTENTION	SELF-LOVING ACTS
Live slowly to detach from achievement-based validation.	Making more time to rest. Having a boundary that every Sunday is for me and I can politely decline any social plans I wish. Having a slow morning routine – waking up and practising moments of joy like going on a walk, grabbing a coffee or pampering myself before I jump into a day at work/school. Cooking my own meals – making nutrition and health a priority instead of hustle culture. Using cooking as a therapeutic practice to listen to my favourite music and hack my happy hormones. Taking up meditation to become more present with myself. Having an evening journal practice or writing letters to myself weekly to enjoy the small wins and document my life for the benefit of my future self.
Simply just learning how to feel comfortable alone.	Go about as normal but prioritise my needs and lifestyle – saying no, communicating my desires and putting myself first unashamedly.

Intention	Self-loving acts
	Exposure therapy – choosing to overdress every day for a week until I no longer fear judgement from others. Taking up a new hobby to change the narrative of having fun from being dependent on others to finding joy alone. Redefining loneliness to find the blessing in solitude. Spending quality time alone – no devices. Going on walks, solo dates, being creative, joining a class or people watching.

What does solitude mean to you?

In terms of being alone, this will mean something different for everybody. You can commit to a complete detox where you resist meeting new people to instead focus that time on yourself. This would be an appropriate choice for someone who's trying to overcome their people-pleasing tendencies or wanting to improve their sense of self without letting other people's perceptions and opinions interfere. This allows you to get to know yourself *as you are* rather than who you are as a friend, colleague or partner. You will still have social time with the people around you but your focus won't be to gain popularity or to impress others. You are shifting away from clubbing every weekend and spending your evenings on dating apps to making time for your self-loving behaviours. It's not a lockdown, just a shift in the time you commit to others versus yourself.

On the other hand, you could just cut out dating while investing in friendships and networking. This is what I did. My biggest struggle was chasing male validation. So I quit clubbing, stopped looking at my DM requests, started dressing for myself and when I felt boredom kicking in, I researched local networking events or started building relationships with girls online, which eventually turned into cute lunches and meet-ups! My main focus was still self-love, but it felt so great to finally find love in others without the dependence. I had so much fun getting to know new people, rediscovering myself in those environments and learning how to build tight-knit friendships that it made what I thought I'd lost with dating laughably insignificant.

Another option is to spend half a year on solitude and the second half carrying out your new self-love practices and applying them to your regular life. We are social creatures and just because you find ease in something alone doesn't mean you'll feel the same in a social setting. Detachment is easy when there's no one taking up all your time. The best way to implement your new mindset and lifestyle is to practise it in the environments that you have previously failed to maintain those standards in.

Personally, after nine months of solitude, I grew comfortable and very hyper-independent. Self-love and solo dating came so naturally to me that I had to incorporate something new to aid my growth journey. So I started partying again at university and making friends with a wider group of people. My energy had significantly changed in the time that I had chosen solitude, and

I felt much more secure and happy in the choices I was making, despite being surrounded by all my previous triggers. I wasn't dressing for anyone's approval, I wasn't flirting with every guy in the bar, I was completely detached and embracing the present moment. My idea worked – after three months, this lifestyle provided a whole new set of lessons, particularly on friendship standards, and that was all thanks to getting back out there with the lessons I had at the time while accepting any mistakes I was about to make.

Whatever you decide, self-sufficiency is at the forefront of how you spend the year. You are your biggest commitment and responsibility. It can feel isolating to embark on changes without having someone to tell, but it is in the process of living life through the good and bad without having someone to hold your hand through it that you will finally build up the strength you always longed for when you would lose yourself because of how someone else decided to treat you. When you sit with the displeasure of going to sleep without a phone call or spending a Friday night alone, your resourcefulness eventually creates way for you to seek the joy in these circumstances. Then, when you finally return to creating connections with others, you can feel assured that no matter which way it ends, you will always have a loving home to return to within yourself. You will never again be tortured by the thought that you are all alone or unlovable because you will have set a foundation which equates every 'heart-breaking loss' to a redirection which you will always, without exception, benefit from.

THE DIFFICULT DAYS

Loneliness is not synonymous with being alone. In fact, you could feel deeply lonely at a dinner table full of friends. This is because loneliness is a feeling, not a state. So, you can have a hundred friends or one, but you will still be susceptible to loneliness if you feel misunderstood and unauthentically seen. Spending a year alone can feel intimidating when you're comparing your journey to others'. When it seems as though everyone's on the same path, and yet you're doing something so painfully abnormal, that can make you doubt why you started in the first place. We often make the mistake of assuming the correct path is the one most followed – that party looks more fun, that couple has the cutest Instagram pictures and that friendship group are always making memories together. But what many fail to realise is most people create a specific outer experience to escape the happenings of their inner world.

People chase popularity and social acceptance from a young age because they fear the status of being 'a loner'. When they find success in their efforts, it has people like you wondering why your life doesn't look as good as theirs. What you don't see is the loneliness they experience because they have been so busy chasing others that they have a complete lack of self. They rely on other people to fill the emptiness they were originally experiencing so they approach these relationships with a desperate need. When you grow attached to what you're supposed to have, look like or who you should be with, you will only ever attract the wrong kind of company – the friendship group that matches your vibrational state and mirrors your insecurities back to you. But when you take the time to transform your loneliness into intentional solitude, you start approaching relationships with confidence, love, genuine care and higher standards. You are operating from a place of want, not need, and that is reflected in the type of people you attract into your life. When you expect the best for yourself and you have done the work to understand the value you can bring to friendships, you won't ever find yourself feeling invisible in a room full of people ever again.

Many make the mistake of associating loneliness with having no one but yourself, but in reality, loneliness is the absence of yourself. The discomfort you feel when sitting alone is the result of avoiding other emotions and thoughts and then having to face them because no one else is there to engage your attention. Once you pay attention to these thoughts and give them the validation and attention they require, being alone no longer feels so daunting. All the companionship, fun and love you crave is already within yourself – you just have to learn how to tap into it. This is achieved by converting loneliness into solitude. It starts with gratitude. You get over your urge to look around at others and think 'why not me?', replacing it with the thought 'I am intentionally alone and I am enjoying every second of this self-discovery so that I get to (not have to) understand and love myself to a greater degree than before.' Not everyone gets the time and ability to do so. So many are fighting to stay in survival mode throughout their life that very few get the chance to pause and take a look at themselves to see what they can improve to make the life to come easier.

CHAPTER SUMMARY

- ☐ Loving yourself is a behaviour, not a feeling. It is a series of choices which separates self-avoiding habits, such as chasing others, with self-acknowledging behaviours, like improving your self-talk and doing your shadow work.
- ☐ Unconditional love should be reserved for yourself. High standards should be set for everyone else in your life. You are the only person who you are guaranteed to be with for the rest of your life – make it a pleasant experience.
- ☐ Being alone means something different for everybody. You can focus solely on your friendships or career or keep all other people in your life to a minimum so you get to know who you are without the presence of other people.

CHAPTER HOMEWORK

- ☐ Complete two solo dates from the bucket list this month (see pages 185–7).
- ☐ Go on a solo date which requires you to stay off your phone for an entire hour.
- ☐ Pick your solo dating intention and complete at least one of the self-loving acts associated with it (see pages 196–8).
- ☐ Schedule an intentional 'lonely' day to practise shifting that feeling into solitude. Loneliness is only a mindset. You get to decide the contentment you can feel in your own space. It is only when you remove the fear of it and embrace your aloneness that it won't feel that bad at all.

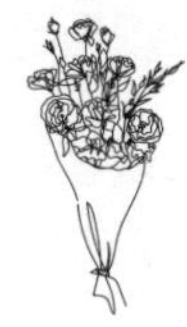

CHAPTER 8:

CONFIDENCE BUILDING

Is having zero insecurities possible?

Insecurities are taught, not formed. We already know the media, societal expectations and trendy beauty standards are the cause of this. While we can't control every piece of media and conversation we are exposed to, we can control our own mindsets.

We are so in our heads all the time that we can forget to live life as we are too distracted by wondering if we look good doing it. I've found it's so normalised for women to insult themselves after taking a photo: 'Ew, I hate that', 'Take that again, my body looks weird', 'That's gross, don't post it'. We can become so used to disrespecting ourselves that we don't even realise it. If a negative response like this has become a natural reaction to simply seeing what you look like then I completely understand why, but it's a problem. This sort of harsh reaction is because you are never actually seeing yourself. You see the way you should be, the way others look, the beauty standard expectations you feel you fall short on and that's why you criticise. What if instead of looking at a photo and hating it because you can only envision the body you wish you had, you started seeing yourself for the way you already are and learned to appreciate it instead?

There's no point in concerning yourself with beauty standards when what one person deems perfect another will find completely unappealing. Plenty of people don't find your celebrity crush in any way attractive but that doesn't invalidate their beauty – it's simply a difference in opinion. Everyone's conflicting opinions cancel each other out, and the most important one is your own. Thus, when you start owning the way you look, act, speak and live, you start believing in your beauty because you're no longer discrediting yourself every waking moment.

We also don't realise that the reason we find others so irresistible is because of their self-confidence. If your favourite celebrity hid themselves away, had awkward body language and refused to put effort into their appearance simply because they didn't see the point there would be nothing to admire. It takes someone to acknowledge the fact they don't fit in, embrace the qualities people criticise and fall in love with themselves regardless to have the whole world fall for them too. At the end of the day, people only criticise what they feel insecure about in themselves. Someone disparaging your body type represents the judgement they have towards themselves. They won't be able to comprehend how someone who looks or acts differently could be so confident in owning their character because they've been so busy trying to live up to everyone else's expectations. People are judging you because they judge themselves. As soon as something they were disparaging about becomes a trend, you'll find they will completely change their view and start praising it.

Happy people don't judge. Confident people don't notice

other peoples 'flaws' or insecurities because they're too busy enjoying their lives. Judgements come from people who are so hyper-aware of things they don't like about themselves that they automatically compare themselves to everyone they come across to see how they measure up. They can't help it – they're so fixated on what they lack with such fear around being 'found out' for it that they are constantly on the lookout for someone 'inferior' to make themselves feel more comfortable. Except the people they choose to compare themselves to usually stand out to them in the first place because they trigger their insecurities. In the imagined social hierarchy they have in their minds, that they use to see where people rank so that they can feel superior, it is those who they are higher than on their imagined scale that are subject to their hatred. At any cost, they will try to pick out someone's 'flaws' and keep bringing attention to them to lower that person's confidence and reassure themselves that they have a higher ranking. You can often tell when you are being subjected to this as it will come in the form of backhanded compliments, gossip and criticism of small details like your skin tone, weight, dress sense, etc. Realising this changed my life. I was only hurt by other people because I was putting them on a pedestal. When I saw that someone being so concerned with bringing you down is essentially them announcing their own self-hatred, I stopped taking everything so personally.

The power in being disliked

It's okay to be disliked. I'm not going to pretend that 'all your haters are your fans' because that's not true. There's no point in assuming every single person must adore you. They won't and that's okay, but it's important to build up a tolerance to the thought of being disliked because so much freedom comes along with it – for one, it allows you to focus on living in your authenticity more. When you get bold in living in your truth knowing people will judge you for it, you filter out those who aren't meant for you, you can find your aligned tribe without doubt and you forfeit your need for external recognition. Not everyone is meant for you so being disliked is never personal. Do you like everyone? No, and nor should you. Only truly connecting with a handful of people is a gift. They are who we need to guide us on the correct path to where we want to be. So, when you don't get along with someone or don't get a good vibe, it's a sign to look elsewhere.

It's the same for your haters. You simply don't align with their beliefs and values, and so you're not meant to be in each other's lives. The only difference is you wouldn't go around being mean just because you didn't like someone, but they do because they're busy fighting their inner battles, so they channel everyday experiences into spiteful energy. You're not unlucky for being disliked or rejected, you are a normal human being who is simply following the life path set out for you and encountering those who do not match your values along the way, thus reinforcing what you desire/dislike, which informs necessary decisions on your life path. If everyone loved you instantly, there would be no growth and no personal discovery to gain. Other people are very influential on our paths to creating the ideal version of ourselves and our lives. Good and bad people are equally important. So, learn to embrace your haters; they teach you more about yourself than you realise.

It's important to mention those who will try to make out that your self-love journey is something to be ashamed of. People will claim you're selfish or self-obsessed. But it's only the most broken of individuals who scream and shout about it. Some of them will be so loud it will convince you everyone's judging you, causing you to dismiss the dozens of people who felt inspired by your energy but didn't comment on it. Negative people are the loudest, while confident people can be silent in their admiration. I remind myself of this when after posting a video online, I start worrying about the hate comments because they're so expressive in their disapproval. But then I remember to recognise that tens of thousands people liked the video without commenting because they never saw an issue with it.

Intrinsic confidence

Confidence and self-love go hand in hand. When you're in love with yourself you wouldn't spend a second of your precious energy trying to pick out faults in another (mostly because it's none of your business how someone else lives their life) and thus lower your own vibration. But people who live life in survival mode, neglecting the inner work and doing everything just to escape their self-directed negative energy, pour real time and energy into humbling others.

To be humble is defined in the Oxford Dictionary as 'having a low estimate of one's importance'. Self-hating people can't stand it when you like yourself because to a person who's so used to self-loathing, of course it's going to appear egotistical. These people get so comfortable in their habits of keeping themselves small that they cannot digest the thought of someone putting themselves out there or appreciating their own beauty. To them, it feels like bragging because they cannot relate. It's funny that haters often try to claim you think you're better than others, and yet a truly confident person would never compete in the first place because they don't see other people's strengths as their weaknesses. They don't feel the need to try to be the smartest or loudest in the room because they're not concerning themselves with other people in the first place. Yet, what these haters don't realise is that trying to bring you down and invalidate your opinions demonstrates that they think their opinion is above yours and thus that they are better than you – projection at its finest.

Feeling differently about yourself with each passing day is a sign that your confidence is coming from the wrong place. Extrinsic confidence is inconsistent and based on conditions (another form of having conditional love for yourself). This means that your most confident phases usually coincide with clear skin, the right outfit, material goods, a higher-paying job, compliments and achieving your goals. If you wonder why you go through days when you suddenly don't feel good enough anymore it's because you've been busy living in a place that doesn't exist. Being in the present comes with accepting that you will never be perfect and not subjecting yourself to such a harsh and impossible standard. It is an act of self-hate to be chasing something to feel good enough – why do you need to be perfect and devoid of flaws to be able to love yourself? You don't need to be doing more because you are not your accomplishments. You can desire to achieve all the goals you want – but without attaching it to your sense of self.

Common habits of the extrinsically confident person include talking about doing self-care and therapy but constantly using excuses to push it back (living in a way that they're too busy for themselves), using work and business as a coping mechanism and feeling lazy when taking time off because they correlate productivity with self-esteem. The reason real self-love is so difficult for this type of person is because it is a slow burner. Self-love can't be measured, tracked or successfully completed. It is a lifelong journey.

When you feel insecure, it's easier to seek out confidence in the things that are easier to strategise and 'win', like achieving goals. It reassures you and makes you feel like a success, whereas self-love lacks this element and that's what makes it feel so hard. Using your appearance and successes as a crutch to feel more confident will fail as soon as you have a day when you don't feel like you look good or you don't achieve what you wanted to, whereas when you base your confidence on who you are internally, no one can get in the way of that. You become untouchable. This is achieved through viewing yourself via your self-defining qualifies: your values, personality, mindset and ability to love. It starts with resilience.

You need to establish security when you are in the process of doing the inner work on the parts of yourself you dislike. That is not to say you will remove them (unless they are toxic) because self-acceptance is a major pillar of self-love. You need to build self-awareness and honour the inner parts you tend to hide away out of insecurity and wounded energy. This confidence comes with moving your attention away from the end result and instead celebrating yourself for doing the hard work in the first place. It is a step that most people skip because of the discomfort that accompanies it. When uncovering difficult parts and insecurities, it's important to build a positive view of these traits in the sense that they are still a part of you and without them, you wouldn't be on this journey in the first place. They are not something to be ashamed of, they are a sign of the life you've lived and the methods you've previously attempted to use in dealing with them.

'Fake it till you make it' was an important tool in my confidence journey. It is the reason I am where I am today. Many look down on this tool as a form of deceiving others and pretending to be something you're not, but I believe it's a powerful way of fulfilling your full potential. You can't become the version of yourself that's full of self-love and confidence by doing the same things that got you where you are today because they clearly have not worked. In order to get your desired result, you have to do a complete identity shift. This tool is not about deception but rather embodying the characteristics you desire until they naturally become a part of you. It's like going to the gym the first time – you're confused, you can't work the machines and you don't know the correct form, but that's not supposed to stop you! You don't quit the gym because you lack knowledge and you think it looks like you're pretending to be good at something you're not. The whole point is to keep practising lifting weights and trying different routines until you gain familiarity and clarity in what works for you – and the same goes for improving your self-esteem.

Your actions are not representative of your self-love. Our actions are mismatches for our mindsets all the time. Self-love is a mindset – the forgiveness, the self-talk, the boundaries, the compassion and the acceptance. The point of balance is achieved when you identify your toxic traits and know you are doing more harm than good in allowing them to continue, while also recognising you are doing what you can at the energetic capacity you are holding each day. You missed a day at the gym? So what? Going to the gym is an action of self-care.

Firstly, you need to stop identifying as the insecure version of yourself. I made the mistake of changing my appearance and assuming it would change the way I felt about myself. While it did get me a lot of dates and compliments, I still felt the same as my 15-year-old awkward self. I had to step out of that mindset and identify as the woman I was growing into. To avoid falling back into the old patterns of my weaker mindset, I challenged myself to look at every day like it was the first day of my life – no baggage, no memory of being insulted, no past. I'd simply wake up and use the resources I had at hand to try to be my best self without allowing what people have said in the past to determine what decisions I make, therefore keeping me trapped in a place of extrinsic confidence.

Then I began focusing on achieving inner confidence. I started looking at the kind of person I was behind closed doors and forced myself to bring her out into the open. This meant no longer doubting my humour, being as loud as I wanted and saying the first things that came to my mind. Was it scary?

Extremely. But I did it anyway because every one of these actions contributed to breaking down the wall of who I should be to love who I already am. All the things I had judged myself so harshly for ended up being accepted by the true friends I found from being myself.

Lastly, I put myself on the pedestal. The version of myself without any embellishments – just who I am at my core. I started seeing so much beauty in my aura, the energy I spread in a room, my impact on others, my ability to stay kind in unkind situations and all my big dreams and beliefs. This solidified such a worthy self-image that I took my power back in social settings. It was no longer about 'will they like me?' but now 'do I like them enough to give them a place in my life?'. I saw myself and my life as a sacred environment that other people had to be worthy of having a place in.

Extrinsic confidence

The 'looking-glass self' describes the process wherein individuals base their sense of self on how they believe others view them, as coined by sociologist Charles Cooley. Using social interaction as a type of 'mirror', people use the judgements they receive from others to measure their own worth, values and behaviour. This is a prime example of extrinsic confidence and external validation. The ultimate answer to unconditional self-confidence is through mastering self-validation. You have to create your own narrative and definitions of beauty instead of letting others do it for you.

Exposure therapy is useful for practising the art of validating yourself. You have to do something you know will be subject to judgement and while you are experiencing all the cringe and embarrassment that comes with it, you change the narrative of those negative opinions into positive ones. The truth is that your negative judgements are only created as a result of years of internalising societal views and becoming a master in predicting how people might perceive you. What you think is 'embarrassing' is a judgement you have inherited from others and now you are using it to judge yourself. So post the video, wear the outfit, go out without makeup, shoot your shot and present that meeting while assuring yourself just how *normal* each of those experiences are. This is when you start to drown out the potential opinions of others to become completely self-referring. You are the only person you are trying to impress so if you put an outfit together, you will go out in it without second-guessing if it's flattering or 'too much' – that's the voices of external validation coming to sabotage you. If you can stay consistent in this practice for 30 days, it will become a habit and you will finally rid yourself of the need to live for others.

It is also crucial to cut out the way you validate other people's opinions on your life. Tendencies to call a friend asking for advice, posting your outfit in the group chat and asking if the guy you're dating is good enough all pushes the narrative that your choices and ability to make the right decision are not enough as they are. When you continue to ask for a second opinion or reassurance, it deepens the hole of mistrusting yourself. Your mindset is the result of the actions you take on a daily basis. Every decision will either confirm a limiting belief or an abundant one.

Let's take body image, for example. You will never escape the feeling of inferiority if you decide to live in a way that supports your fear of gaining weight or having the wrong body type, e.g. restricting yourself, counting calories, online comparison, pointing out every fold and roll on your stomach. Self-love starts to grow when your decisions turn into eating intuitively because your body is simply a vessel, not a measure of your worthiness, and you eating the food you enjoy creates memories not anxiety. Beauty is not a one-size-fits-all trait. You could fulfil every possible standard you dream of for yourself and there would still be people who deem you unattractive and unworthy. It is a game you can never win because the dice will never be in your hands. Take your power back by choosing an inner monologue that honours who you are as you are in this moment, so you don't spend your lifetime chasing an ideal that was created by other people rather than learning how to be your source of admiration.

CHAPTER SUMMARY

- [ ] Insecurities are taught, not formed. While we cannot prevent this, we can alter the choices we make each day to start appreciating ourselves rather than refusing to see who we are because we are too busy fixating on who we should be.
- [ ] Happy people don't judge. There's no point in paying attention to criticism when it's coming from people whose lives have gone beyond a point of misery that they have no choice but to start focusing on yours instead.
- [ ] Embrace the experience of being disliked because it liberates you. You gain more clarity on who your people are and what you should be doing. How will you ever know what is truly meant for you when you are performing for others and attracting energies that have nothing to do with the most authentic version of you?
- [ ] Extrinsic confidence comes from external factors like clothes, money and accomplishments whereas intrinsic confidence comes from who you are as a person. The latter is the only way to have an unbreakably strong self-esteem.
- [ ] Embodying the characteristics you want until they naturally become a part of you isn't 'fake', it's the only way to improve yourself. You can't get to a new destination by continuing on the same old road.

CHAPTER HOMEWORK

- [ ] Learn how to validate yourself. Stop yourself in moments of seeking reassurance for others and challenge yourself to make decisions based on your natural instinct every day for a week. You'll find that there was nothing inherently wrong with your ideas in the first place.
- [ ] The only way to build intrinsic confidence is by honouring your insecurity. You have to change the way you define these parts of yourself. It is self-harming to label parts of yourself as 'bad'. Reframe the narrative of your social skills or facial features to ones that celebrate them.

PART THREE:

REAWAKENING

Living with your new self-love mindset

CHAPTER 9:

VALENTINE'S DAY WILL BE YOUR FAVOURITE EVENT

Life is the occasion

As a serial dater, I never experienced the struggle of feeling haunted by aloneness on Valentine's Day. And then my first single Valentine's Day was in my self-love year. I had set the intention to fall in love with myself, and because of this mindset, I felt excited about planning the way I would show up for myself after years of being dependent on somebody else to make me feel loved.

Since that day in 2021, I have made 14 February my favourite day of the year. In the years that followed, I had dinner at fancy restaurants alone while surrounded by couples and spent the entire day doing my favourite things and treating myself amid the romance around me. Even now, as I've been in a relationship for the last year, I continue to make extra effort in celebrating the love I have for myself weekly, but especially on Valentine's Day.

A relationship is not the destination of your self-love journey – this is ongoing and not to be abandoned as your circumstances change. Loving yourself to new heights as your romantic relationship progresses allows you to maintain detachment and independence so you never crumble at the actions of another ever again. You can only feel sad on Valentine's Day if you are running away from yourself. Only you can provide what you need (love, confidence, validation, comfort, reassurance, understanding, attention), so why do we always crave someone else on Valentine's Day to fix the emptiness we feel in ourselves?

It's okay to desire a relationship but hating the idea of Valentine's Day because you haven't found the person who will make everything better only signals the work you need to do to show up for yourself. Be thankful for who you are now rather than wishing for versions of yourself who don't exist yet. You are ignoring the gift of commitment and time you have all to yourself if you are in pursuit of a lifestyle that will inevitably come, while the timer is ticking on the life you're living now. You don't have to have your dream life for it to be worthy of celebration, just the fact that your singlehood is temporary warrants appreciation enough. It is the person you are now who gets you what you have always wanted, so why reject her when she holds the power to forge the path you are about to walk upon? The kinder you treat her, the better she will be at choosing the right partner at the right time. If you engage in sorrow at not having found your person, you create a future version of yourself that is more likely to settle and pick *anyone* to love because of the fear and rejection you will associate with being alone for any longer.

What if this is your last Valentine's alone? What if someone told you every 14 February for the rest of your life would be spent celebrating the love you have with another person and you looked back at all the moments you neglected showering yourself with love, when you had no idea that opportunity was going to be taken away so soon? How would you spend your time right now if you knew your soulmate was on their way? Would you be more present? Would you focus on your growth? Would you date without worry? Just the assurance that you would find your partner soon would completely transform the way you view your singlehood. We're not sad because we're alone, we're sad because we assume we'll be alone forever. Assuming that you won't get the relationship you desire reflects a limiting belief system of your capabilities and worth. Your assumptions and feelings do not accurately portray what will happen in your life. They are merely a projection of your own self-perception. Sadness as a single on Valentine's Day is unheard of when you're filled with self-love because you're always living in the thought that your singlehood is a gift and you act accordingly every single day.

Even if you never meet your person, this is a holiday that celebrates love – the problem we encounter is the fixation on *romantic* love. There are so many forms of love – friendship, family, mankind, self. Yet we fail to see the love we already have in our lives because there's only one form of love promoted on this day. While others may not adjust their viewpoint, it's down to you to change the narrative of a day that could easily have you wallowing in self-pity to one that makes you thankful in self-love instead. Maybe it's not that 'there aren't enough good men in the world', it's 'the circumstances of my current life reflect the necessary timing of it. When I'm meant to have something, I will see it clearly'. Maybe it's not that nobody likes you, but that you don't like everybody and that is something to be celebrated, especially on a day that pressures so many people to find a date just to *have* somebody.

After mastering a mindset of self-love, Valentine's Day felt like another birthday to me. Instead of celebrating turning another year older and reflecting on the life I've lived, this day became a celebration of the courage I had for starting a relationship with myself. This journey didn't begin when I was born but rather in the middle of my life, yet it felt like a re-birth. It completely altered the way I look at the life I experience and the way I treat myself – I am a completely different person because of it. Valentine's Day marks another year to reflect on the ways I showed up for myself, the solo dates I went on, the things I refused to settle for and the growth I experienced in improving how I handled all areas of my life.

It's excitingly challenging too. As soon as February arrives, my yearly self-reflection begins and I think of all the ways I can implement the new confidence I've developed since the previous Valentine's Day to make the next one even more extravagant for myself. When you love yourself, you also love to see others rightfully being loved. The sight of cute pictures online or public displays of affection doesn't irritate you but rather reminds you of the love that is abundant and available all around you. It's not a sign of your lack but rather all the excitement that is to come, and, in the meantime, you are enjoying who you are without having to be on the edge of your seat just waiting to be saved by somebody else.

But this isn't just reserved for Valentine's Day. Self-love is something to be practised every single day. Self-love develops from the way you show up in every mundane moment of your life, in every decision you make and in every action you take. It doesn't require excessive planning or thought. It can be as simple as buying the nice dishware or clothing and deciding to use it as you please instead of saving it 'for a special occasion' – because life itself *is the occasion*. Every day you wake up and get to be *you* is a day to be celebrated. It's not about having somewhere fancy to go, just being alive is reason enough. Every day offers the gift of mystery – you have no idea what you're about to learn, which places you could discover, what people you could meet or how much change this day will bring to your life as a whole – isn't that something to get dressed up for?!

When you love yourself, you are more capable of living life to the fullest because your focus is wholeheartedly on yourself. As a default, many of us wonder what we could have, or what other people are doing, and how we measure up to them in comparison. We're so stressed about whether we're doing well enough or what the next best steps are, that we often forget to give recognition to the person we were today, and that is where the self-love lies. It's in focusing on the 24 hours in front of you instead of stressing about the entire week ahead – when only today exists in your view, all you can do is pour every ounce of your energy and effort into making it a great one.

There's no opportunity or 'better day' to wait for. You are taking advantage of every second you have in front of you instead of letting it pass by in search for some imagined ideal. It's learning to build acceptance of what your circumstances are without needing to complain or wish for change because the change is on its way already. It's up to you to build gratitude for what you have now so that you have the ability to attract better energies into your life. There's no chance of falling back into comparison spirals when your view is suddenly pushed towards rays of sun, blooming trees, strangers in love, the taste of coffee and enjoying new food. When you are so consumed by just getting through the day or attaching happiness to a moment in the future, you are sacrificing the power you have over your life in the present. As a result, you continue to attract the same level of scarcity because that's all you choose to focus on, creating a cycle of the same old dissatisfaction and eventually disapproval to yourself.

Sure, there will be days when you feel on top of the world and days when you are bored out of your mind with the reading, early nights, healthy foods and stable routines. No one's texting you, your circle is smaller than ever and you feel the urge to go back to old comforts. This is normal. What helps you stay consistent in this new phase of your life is romanticisation. You aren't meant to ignore your feelings or invalidate yourself. This technique prioritises creating consistent small wins that give you the inner love and satisfaction that encourages you to keep going among all the sacrifices. Changing the narrative is an effective method of doing this; it means actively deciding what you allow to ruin or better your day. Next time you're delayed on a train, use it as an opportunity to catch up on your reading or call an old friend. When you get ready just for your plans to get cancelled, rise to the spontaneity that comes with the situation and become a tourist in your own city. In annoying situations like being stuck in traffic, you get to make the best out of a bad situation. Similarly, you get to choose when to construct your own moments of joy.

I spent so many years living life in black and white mode.

I woke up and just tried to get through the day. I tolerated the conversations I was having. I accepted the treatment I was getting. I was pushing through the responsibilities that were given to me and I would drag myself through each day just trying to get to the end of it. The only thing that remotely made me feel some sense of hope was the idea of a better future. When I could call someplace my home, when I had freedom, passion, friends and happiness. But in what timeline? And how? What did happiness even mean to me? Just the fantasy of a better life *someday* was enough of a temporary dopamine hit to keep me going – yet I was doing nothing to get there.

I finally realised that happiness isn't found, it's created. It is not dependent on the type of life you lead but the type of life you choose to receive. Looking towards the future as an idea of happiness is the same as seeking confidence from external validation – you are always looking for things outside yourself. Even after I had undone the years of insecurity and trauma while combining it with quality time alone, I was left stuck on how to love myself in a life I hated. But I remembered how self-discovery was such a key part of my journey to loving myself because I was paying more attention to every insignificant detail of who I was and how I was growing. It was then I realised that self-discovery isn't just scheduling time for tests to learn about yourself, it is achieved through life experience and the way you craft it. So, I started purposefully inserting the colour back into my life. I planned a personal happiness ritual every single morning that would make me leap out of bed in elation. I'd blast some feel-good music, dance unskilfully as if I was in a movie and look at my to-do list for the day as dozens of chances to evolve took shape before me. I started planning my weeks in advance so that I could schedule something to look forward to in every single one. Whether it was a walk at sunset, a movie night or a DIY project – every day became an event. I didn't have to wait for birthdays or Christmas because now I could wake up every day with the purpose of creating my own happiness.

DAILY ROUTINE . . .

One of the biggest factors that helped in embracing my new lifestyle as someone filled with self-love was the 'how can I make this moment as *enjoyable* as possible?' mindset. Meaning every regular moment became one of opportunity. Here are some examples of how to achieve this mindset:

THE MINDSET OF THE AVERAGE PERSON ...	... AND OF SOMEONE FILLED WITH SELF-LOVE
Wake up 20 minutes before you have to leave for work. Run around in a panic trying to get dressed and remember your things. Leave home in a hurry, probably on an empty stomach, dreading the day ahead.	Wake up two hours before you have to leave for work. Get out of bed immediately in your excitement to begin your morning rituals. The first starts with relaxation. Make your favourite breakfast/coffee, read a book, listen to music or watch the sunrise – whatever lights you up because joy is the priority here. Afterwards, try to do some exercise – a HIIT workout, yoga or a quick walk to hack your happy hormones. Get ready for work at a gentle pace after starting the day on your own terms. Put effort into your outfit and try a new makeup look that you've saved on your phone to bring new energy into an otherwise normal day.
Start your daily commute while scrolling on your phone and thinking of all the ways yet another workday is about to drain you. Fall into a daydream of all the things	As your mood is enhanced with the new appearance you're experimenting with, you act like the main character with the playlist you have carefully curated as

THE MINDSET OF THE AVERAGE PERSON . . .	. . . AND OF SOMEONE FILLED WITH SELF-LOVE
you wish you could be doing and let them frustrate you out of the realisation it's all 'unrealistic'. Then return to trying to self-soothe in preparation for yet another day in the repetitive cycle of survival that is your life.	the soundtrack to your life. These songs uplift you and transform the feeling of an otherwise boring commute. As you travel, you people watch, try to find new things in your surroundings and embrace being in the present because anything could happen – you never know what each day could bring or who you might meet or what you could discover.
Start your daily work tasks while thinking of all the places you'd rather be. Scroll on social media in your breaks to live vicariously through others and their seemingly perfect lives. Return to work feeling slightly more hopeless and start the countdown to when you can finally go back to your bed.	Start your daily work tasks while reassuring yourself of the time you prayed for this moment in your life. You have a job, you're making money, you're no longer in the stress that was trying to find employment. Even if it's not something that fulfils you, you have made your younger self proud in taking these steps so far. In your breaks, take time away from your screens, enjoy your food and go for a walk.

THE MINDSET OF THE AVERAGE PERSON . . .	. . . AND OF SOMEONE FILLED WITH SELF-LOVE
	Try to connect with your co-workers to improve your confidence, learn more skills on the job or romanticise being the corporate movie character you always looked up to.
Finally, make your way home, throw some leftovers together and watch TV until you have to go to bed. Get into bed and scroll to try and grab some control of your day until 2am. Then fall asleep knowing you'll be sleep deprived in the morning and do the same routine all over again in the morning.	Text your friends to organise a meetup after work or simply have a Facetime. Social time is important to feel connected in a hectic world – this will maintain your mental health. Play some jazz music, make a girly drink, light some candles and make a delicious dish of pasta then sit back and indulge while watching your favourite movie. Even the basic chores in life can be made into an event. Afterwards, spend 20 minutes doing a face mask or an at-home pedicure. You deserve these little moments of indulgence and luxury even if you have to make them yourself.

CHAPTER SUMMARY

- ☐ Valentine's Day becomes your favourite event when you redefine it on your own terms. Love is abundant in all areas of life, especially within yourself.
- ☐ Shaming yourself for being single for 'too long' only impairs your ability to make the right decisions later down the line. The more you feel insecure about being alone, the more you'll feel pressured into rushing into something that isn't right for you. Releasing the fear of rejection and isolation is the kindest act of love you can do for your future self so that she is fearless in her standard and boundary setting.
- ☐ What if this was your last year or day single? How would you spend it, knowing you'd never again experience the gifts this phase of your life has to offer? Fill yourself with that gratitude now. The only reason you feel sad is because you assume singlehood is forever, not because singlehood lacks joy.
- ☐ Self-love can be practised in the same way every day by romanticising your life. Change the narrative of your days by deciding how you perceive each moment and plan ahead to schedule something to look forward to every day. When you wake up, your mind isn't on the amount of work you have to do or what you lack, it's on how you're going to fulfil your purpose of trying to have a good day.

CHAPTER HOMEWORK

- ☐ Bring Valentine's Day energy into today. Take yourself on a date, have a self-care night, take a day off from everything or just be gentler to yourself.
- ☐ Try to soak up every bit of happiness a 'mundane' moment could create, e.g. lighting candles, dancing to your favourite throwback songs or reading a new book.
- ☐ Shift your morning routine to be more intentional with your joy by using at least one of the routines written in the table on pages 229–31.

CHAPTER 10:

SETTING BOUNDARIES TO SERVE YOURSELF

Prioritising peace over perception

Once you've mastered self-love, your interactions with everyone around you will transform. Your focus will finally be removed from what other people think of you and whether you're likeable to fixating on your own best interest. That's not to say you're strictly a self-serving person. One of the main reasons why boundaries are so important is that they ensure your cup is full and your energy is protected so that you are in a better position to show up for the *deserving* people around you without feeling resentful. Learning your worth will have you placing yourself on the pedestal and fearlessly saying no as you wish.

Boundaries aren't about putting people in their place – they're actually not about other people at all – their sole purpose is for you to take responsibility for your 'spiritual hygiene'. This includes where you spend your energy, how much of it you give away and what energies you surround yourself with.

It also deals with removing blockages when it comes to your mental health and belief systems. An example of this is a person who wholeheartedly loves themselves would never date without setting standards or make friends with someone for the sake of having company. They consistently evaluate what does and does not serve them so that they can act accordingly to create a more accomplished life for themselves.

When your focus is on the external, you're so determined to control people's perceptions of you that you lose control of the experiences you receive. You are allowing anyone to have access to you and you're worse off because of it. Boundaries are things you action; you're not trying to change anyone's behaviour by repeating your boundaries verbally and you remove yourself from the relationship or situation altogether if someone continues to cross the line that you clearly communicated *once*. There must be a consequence – it is vital for your self-protection.

FRIENDSHIPS

Aside from the very basic requirements of loyalty, respect and affection, friendship boundaries are severely overlooked. There are so many issues that lead to the breakdown of a friendship and a breakdown in your personal life when you're not carefully assessing the people who try to enter your life.

Let's take the energy vampire as an example. The energy vampire friend will constantly emotionally dump on you, always vent about drama, victimise themselves and very rarely gives you the chance to speak. You are treated as their personal diary, being filled with pages and pages of intense emotional release, thus leaving your own energy depleted. You often leave these interactions feeling drained, heavy-hearted and exhausted.

This is similar to the friend who treats you as a romantic partner. It's a co-dependent concoction that lacks privacy, personal space and independence. Your friend sees you as someone who fixes them, rather than appreciating the value in just getting to spend time with you. There's so much expectation, which strips you of your ability to grow the relationship you have with yourself because you're constantly mothering somebody else. Once again, you have to pour so much energy into someone else that it leaves you very little to give yourself.

Not to mention the pity party friend. They will seem harmless at first as they innocently joke about their shortcomings in their usual self-deprecating way. They will shower you with compliments and practically fall in love with you from the second you meet. Many people see it as a green flag but it's actually the most dangerous sign of all. How can someone obsess over you when they don't even know you yet? This is where their true intentions start coming to light. You are more likely to find a healthy and secure friendship with someone who takes it slow in evaluating whether you're a good fit for their life too. They have enough standards in place and they are aware enough of their worth that they're not desperate to mingle with just anybody. The people who act infatuated with you from the second you meet usually turn out to be the jealous ones down the road. They can't contain themselves in putting you on a pedestal above them and while you think it's sweet the closer they get to you, they just find more to envy. At some point, that once innocent friendship typically leads to betrayal.

I experienced every one of these friendships and it was my own fault. I was so unsure of my worth that I took somebody else liking me at face value and dove straight into a friendship with them. As someone so naturally introverted, I found it difficult to make friends, so I left the ball in others' court to sort of adopt me into their lives – and I was happy enough to be picked. There was no filtering process applied to the people I was surrounding myself with and that meant I was burned by people I thought I could trust one too many times.

After years of these lessons, I learned that you avoid getting into these entanglements completely by using your self-love to justify your high standards. Gone are the days of worrying if I'm being too picky because I'm confident in the fact that being liked isn't something to be impressed by, it's a given. Someone being nice to you is basic human decency. Having a fun time doesn't even begin to show the extent of someone's character. So, I started to construct my personal list of friendship standards. Top of the list was positive self-esteem. I am fully aware that confidence is a lifelong journey and I would never expect anyone to be rid of their problems, but I do expect them to meet me where I've met myself. I have had the self-respect to work through my triggers and insecurities so that I don't compare myself with others. If I can do it for myself, why would I settle for someone who doesn't align with me in friendship? Someone can be kind and reciprocal with you, but still their insecurity risks jealousy, resentment and competition overtime – don't threaten your spiritual hygiene by feeling sorry for them.

Conversation quality is also a must. If I don't walk away from a meet-up feeling inspired, joyful or energised, what was the point? When you get so used to your own company, you don't settle for mediocre interaction. Mindset and influence is also very important to me. Personally, I like to surround myself with ambitious women because that is the life path I'm on. You might want to seek out spiritually enlightened friends or people who value their wellness.

Don't forget that bad influence friends don't just come in the form of those who encourage you to drink too much or put you in unsafe situations; they are also the kind of people who hold you back from your desires because their mind hasn't caught up yet. People don't have to be 'bad' for you to refuse friendship with them. Just someone being too small-minded is a good enough reason to keep your space. Why would you sabotage yourself by accepting energy that doesn't match yours when there are friends who would listen to your dreams and push you to dream even bigger?

Lastly, I question whether I'm satisfied with the way they show up for me. This will be different for everyone. I don't mind when my friends don't text me but if that's an important form of effort you need in friendship then it's your responsibility to communicate that, and if someone isn't willing to do that for you, don't hurt yourself by continuing to seek companionship from a person who has already shown you who they are. You owe it to yourself to make peace with their absence in your life instead of compromising your boundaries for the sake of accepting their disrespect.

DATING

When it comes to romantic connections, the way you treat yourself manifests the way you will be treated. When you lean towards mirroring your partner in the hope of being easy-going and lovable, you forfeit any form of boundaries. Inevitably, they will then start to see that you essentially let them take you for granted, a power imbalance forms and their respect for you starts to crumble.

Boundaries are more than just communicating what you do and do not like. Boundaries represent the relationship you have with yourself. I've found that I rarely need to verbally communicate my needs when dating because my actions do all the talking. I already buy myself flowers, I make my weekly solo dates a commitment, my career comes first, I have a strict routine and I stay consistent in the type of lifestyle I live – these act as boundaries for the way I expect to be treated because if this is what I provide to myself, why would I settle for a low-effort partner who can't match the love I'm already filled with?

An example for me is not responding to texts right away. I'm not a big texter and I like to focus solely on my work between the hours of nine and five so I continue this habit even when I'm dating so I can enforce those boundaries I have set for myself. I used to make the mistake of altering my desires to fit the needs of another. I would respond to texts quickly, finish work earlier and wait around for them. In living my life this way, I was practically encouraging my date to take comfort in the lack of needs he had to meet because I was visibly doing all the chasing.

When you love yourself, you don't wait for problems to arise to communicate your boundaries because you were already open in saying what you need, why you feel that way and how you would respond if a need wasn't met. This isn't about changing or punishing them, it's about refusing to change any part of yourself for the purpose of pleasing someone else. There's also no need to control what they do; you stay for however long this bond meets your needs because you love yourself enough to accept the possibility of distance and know you'll be okay alone in the meantime, so there's no fear in saying the wrong thing or being too harsh in your standards. This is also how you avoid getting 'stuck' in situationships that turn into a prison of your own making. It's as simple as openly talking about your desire for a serious relationship or what you expect the dating timeline to look like. There is no pressure involved. You have the relief in knowing you've been clear in what you want and if their actions fail to follow suit then you have all the reassurance in knowing they weren't right for you and you saved six months of your life that otherwise would have been spent waiting for someone to get the hint. Dating is not about going along with the flow. It's being so upfront about what you want to get out of it that you have the courage to be left alone in the process, because you're certain in the knowledge you will meet someone who goes above and beyond your 'high' standards.

FAMILY

Familial validation is a type of external validation that is particularly difficult to escape from. This is because the expectations you feel you must meet have been instilled in you from the moment you were born. So it feels almost natural to play life according to your family's rule book. How could you even start to detach from their opinions when they taught you which opinions to have? The reason setting boundaries with our family is so uncomfortable is because we're more likely to be people pleasers in a familial environment. The way we were raised determines the adults we grow into by default. After that, it is down to our own personal development to undo the teachings that have been holding us back.

Getting approval from primary caregivers when we are children provides us with our only source of validation in our formative years because our parents or parental figures are the only people we seek love from. So repeated criticism from these figures or simply a lack of validation makes us doubt ourselves and encourages people pleasing tendencies. We can overcompensate out of fear we'll be rejected and that creates our fear of setting boundaries as we grow older because we were raised to predict our parents' reactions, perform for love and keep the peace.

As an adult, trying to impress your family members keeps you stagnant in your self-growth journey. You are succumbing to ideals they have held onto their entire lives rather than identifying and living according to the values you have set for yourself. Your family members, just like every other person in your life, view you through a completely different lens that is solely based on their own traumas, lessons, teachings, values and life experiences. Your mum and dad will see you differently to each other, and the same goes for your siblings and grandparents. Their rules are simply a reflection of the standards they hold for themselves and those that they were taught to uphold – they are merely repeating what they know.

Establishing self-love will cause your family dynamic to change. As you live with this new mindset, you finally step into your power and for a lot of dysfunctional families, this can upset their balance of control over you. In many cases, when you are reawakened in your sense of self, you finally gain clarity in the inaccuracy of who your family declared you were. People can only view you in a way that suits them and the second you outgrow the perception they had of you, tensions can start to rise. You may experience accusations that you are changing for the worse and being disrespectful, or family members generally express their disapproval of who you're becoming. This is where boundaries become more important than ever.

Practising self-love becomes increasingly challenging when you are faced with the opinions of people who have internalised a previous version of you. It is easy to fall back into old patterns, behaviours and coping mechanisms because your personality in the environment your unhealed self grew up in feels so familiar. Growing is easy when it's in a new environment, by yourself and removed from triggers because you don't associate with old comforts – it's like turning a fresh page. But being around family is a constant reminder of who you used to be as well as who they wanted you to be.

Family members can continue to push the narrative or treat you in a way that makes moving backwards feel like the easier option because it makes them feel more comfortable. Setting boundaries is your opportunity to solidify your new mindset in the places your old self is still attached to. Bringing your new behaviours and values into that environment can remove the mental presence of your previous self by healing a fear of being seen. This can be achieved by speaking up when you feel disrespected and explaining why you stand confidently in your decision making – not for approval, but acceptance. Once you have communicated the way you would like to be spoken to and treated, you need to assess if someone is capable of seeing another perspective and holding space for that kind of conversation. If they can't, it is in your own best interest to protect your peace. For some people, this looks like distancing themselves from their family. Or it is maybe a chance to challenge your urge to people please as you continue to spend time with those who don't understand you, while still living in your truth.

Self-love is letting go of your need to be understood and validated because you already give this to yourself. When you do, you remain peaceful while maintaining familial relationships and you meet your parents where they have met themselves. You resist defending your viewpoint because you value your self-care and keeping your emotional stress at bay first and foremost. There's no point trying to converse with someone who isn't really listening. When you master this mindset, it's an example of setting the boundary with yourself.

SETTING BOUNDARIES WITH YOURSELF

Setting boundaries with yourself is how you retain the love and peace within your life. Although boundaries with others are important for being truthful in your relationships and actively practising your standards to determine who is and isn't meant for you, we cannot control other people. We simply communicate what we need and allow them to respond in the way they wish before we decide how to alter our presence and behaviour as a consequence of their chosen action. When it comes to setting boundaries with ourselves, we are in the driver's seat with full control. This is the highest form of self-love. It's doing what you say you're going to, when you're going to do it.

Procrastination and postponing the plans you have for yourself are no longer an option. You now regularly conduct weekly or monthly personal reviews on yourself. This is when you reflect on the progress you've made in your growth, career or relationships. Upon reflection, you start to set boundaries so that you can make the necessary improvements you desire to step into the highest version of yourself.

For example, I am writing this at the end of a month that was spent working overtime with poor sleep quality, little scheduling for my own enjoyment and a complete imbalance with my wellbeing habits. My new boundary is to prioritise having a work–life balance. It's common for a lot of people to set little goals like these when they notice new problems in their life – but action must follow suit. A self-boundary is incomplete and futile without action because of the control you possess. If it goes untested, you're still engaging in a neglectful relationship with yourself. Therefore, it's important to action your boundary by building a weekly schedule in advance that honours your mental health and balances all areas of your life so you don't risk burning out or neglecting giving love back to yourself. This process can include scheduling social time ahead, booking solo date reservations and planning activities or rest time that is non-negotiable and uncancellable.

Another form of setting self-boundaries is letting people be wrong about you. This is where you finally free yourself from so much self-directed pain. We tend to forget that our emotions aren't the result of other people's actions, but rather ourselves. We get to decide how and when we feel – feeling distraught by what someone else says is a decision we have made. When it comes to detaching from others and dealing with difficult relationships, you have to show up for yourself through emotional regulation. This is done by making it a habit to step back in every situation to choose what emotional reaction is best suited to your needs, rather than the severity of the situation itself. You notice how you feel, you hold space for it and accept it, but you leave the situation with the intention to walk it off, journal or listen to music to take back control of what could have been a voluntary deterioration of your wellbeing and possibly self-perception.

Once you've started to commit to your needs no matter what, let go of what doesn't serve you and prioritise peace over reaction, the most important boundary of all is how you choose to treat yourself. Going forward, you will never allow yourself to place such harsh expectations on what it takes to feel worthy, because its already unconditional. You will never have to perform to be worthy of your own praise again. You value the mistakes and the life experience that come with them and so you self-soothe throughout, instead of filling with regret and what ifs. You don't wonder what life would be like if only you were 'better' because there's already so much to love and appreciate about yourself. So why wouldn't you run to comfort yourself in times of suffering? It's the most self-appreciating act of all.

EVERYBODY ELSE

Setting boundaries doesn't stop with your loved ones. Here are some phrases that can help meet your needs when it comes to co-workers, strangers and everyone else.

Boundary setting phrases:

- 'I need time to myself.'
- 'I don't have the capacity for that right now.'
- 'That doesn't work for me, let's compromise.'
- 'I won't be able to attend but thank you for the invite.'
- 'I'm not comfortable discussing that.'
- 'My schedule is full right now, I will reach out to reschedule soon.'
- 'I won't engage in this conversation if you continue to disrespect me.'
- 'I'm grateful for your advice but I'm confident in my decision.'
- 'Can you explain further so I can understand your perspective on this better?'
- 'It's necessary that I prioritise my mental health above all else right now.'
- 'I don't like it when you ____. I'd appreciate it if you respected my feelings on this.'
- 'No.'

CHAPTER SUMMARY

- [ ] Boundary setting is about you, not others. Its purpose is for you to maintain good spiritual hygiene so that you can live a life full of value and minimal depletion.
- [ ] Spiritual hygiene is focusing on evaluating what energy does and doesn't serve the life and self you're working towards. You no longer tolerate what's given to you, you actively create your surroundings.
- [ ] Friendship standards go further than kindness, loyalty, respect and similarity. Do your minds align? Does this person push you further on your most aligned path? Are they a good influence? Are your conversations energising? Do they have good self-esteem?
- [ ] When you fall in love with your own company, you stop holding space for just anybody that wants it for the sake of having people in your life.
- [ ] Boundaries aren't just verbal. The way you live your life and stand firm in your decisions around other people communicates your boundaries without you having to say anything.
- [ ] This process isn't about changing or controlling others, it's about refusing to change parts of yourself to fit their preferences.
- [ ] Setting boundaries with yourself is equally as important, but here you have full control. Not only do you need to decide how you will act and feel for the betterment of yourself, but keep accountable in actioning these decisions.

CHAPTER HOMEWORK

- ☐ Journal about something you're feeling badly about – it could be a work task, something you did or an argument you had. Once you've had that emotional release, practise emotional regulation by detaching from the situation and deciding how you want to feel about it rather than allowing the feeling to control you. Get back in the driver's seat in your life by actioning this self-boundary so your days are no longer ruined by attachment to external situations.
- ☐ Write out a list of your friendship standards and start visualising having people in your life that meet every one effortlessly. The clearer you can imagine it, the more you can remove the need to settle for less than out of fear of it being 'realistic'.
- ☐ Set out your non-negotiable dating habits. Take a look at how you like to spend your social time and your alone time and start maintaining those desires while building a life with another person so your world doesn't revolve around them and they gain more understanding of your boundaries.

CHAPTER 11:

DATING WITH SELF-LOVE

'I love you, but I love me more'

THE DATING TRANSFORMATION

Dating used to be an ego boost. A man texting me or showing any form of interest lit me up, whereas when I went months without going on a date, I felt smaller than ever and as if my life was incomplete and 'unsuccessful'. All because I was dating to escape myself. I preferred the idea of who I became as a girlfriend and object of desire. I could finally separate myself from the multitude of insecurities I carried to become what my partner saw me as. I defined myself through their opinions and actions towards me. Not only did this worsen my self-esteem over time, because I took distance and arguments personally, but I became emotionally dependant on another person. A lot of my happiness relied on their behaviour towards me. Of course, this did more harm than good for my self-perception as all of this was unpredictable and largely out of my control.

Not only that, but, as a result, I consistently attracted low-value men into my life.

The biggest factor that determines whether a man is high-or low-value is how much they add to your life – in other words, the amount of value they provide when dating you. Low-value men aren't bad people necessarily, but their priorities are in a much different place to the guy who is able to give you what you deserve in a relationship. Low-value men tend to have little emotional intelligence and therefore not much control over their likely fluctuating and confusing feelings. This shows up in various behaviours – for example, they likely struggle with commitment, lack clarity on what they want so tend to go after just about anyone, have little self-awareness, make no effort in self-development, have no personal drive so they live on immediate gratification, can be people pleasers and show jealous and needy traits around women because of their insecure attachment styles. This type of man was drawn to me like a magnet because I was in the habit of putting men and their opinions of me on a pedestal.

Low-value men seek out women who do the chasing and give away their power because they too seek validation and have a dependant self-esteem. When a woman lacks self-love, she becomes a big shiny sign that reads 'easily impressed and free to treat as you please'. This is a low-value man's gold mine because all of his negative traits become invisible and his low-effort ways are celebrated. This is because a person who lacks self-love doesn't deem themselves worthy of the big gestures and acts of love. It feels unfamiliar to them or they feel like a burden at the idea of receiving them. When you struggle to love yourself small efforts from someone else feel huge because they're unexpected and presumably undeserved. Even though these small acts don't even touch the surface of the love you could be receiving from the right person. A high-value man may not become involved with a woman who lacks self-love because they're not an energetic match. You only attract those that are vibrating at the same frequency as you. Insecure women will attract low-value men and high-value men will attract confident women who know their worth because they perceive themselves and the world in a similar way.

A high-value man sets standards for his life, knows exactly what he wants and acts accordingly. He will chase his goals over meaningless relationships and has no time to entertain every attractive woman he meets because he protects his energy. He is confident in knowing his value and wouldn't give it out to just anyone. He takes good care of himself and has enough self-love to focus on his wellbeing and healing. Most importantly, he values *being a boyfriend* instead of just wanting a girlfriend. This shows in his efforts to provide for his partner as a result of his emotional intelligence and ambition for pursuing the woman that meets his standards. He has an internal locus of control and so he takes pride in maintaining his relationship rather than feeling entitled to it and growing lazy in how he treats his partner over time.

Once you have entered your self-love era, you start to encompass traits of high self-esteem and spiritual hygiene, making you an energetic match for high-value dating experiences. A secure and confident man is not a win – it is your bare minimum. Similarly, you will start to craft your new definition of your bare minimum – also known as your non-negotiable requirements. You may well need to stop being influenced by other people's ideas of what is realistic so you can better identify your own needs. Even though you're exclusively attracting high-value men into your life, healthy relationships are not necessarily automatic. High-value men will still need to be assessed and independence remains an important aspect of your life, but now the selection of men you come into contact with are elevated and consequently your standards must follow that same growth process.

After spending a year single and working on myself, I re-entered the dating world with so much self-love that I became incapable of having bad dating experiences. I still came across unsuitable matches of course, but being mistreated was a thing of the past. This is a natural outcome of the self-love journey because when you pour so much love into yourself, men must go overboard to bring something to the table that you haven't. When you don't provide for yourself, you jump for joy at the bare minimum – your only standard is your last dating experience. So, if your ex gave you 10 per cent and your new partner gives you 15 per cent, you'd think you found the perfect catch when there's still 75 per cent of high-value love being withheld from you *and you don't even know it*. Provide that 100 per cent to yourself.

GIVE YOURSELF PRINCESS TREATMENT

Giving yourself the love you crave is the most efficient way to ensure you never settle for less than you deserve again. For me, this transformation started with shifting my mindset. I was no longer escaping my life but fully immersed and enjoying every second of it – if someone told me I would still be single in five years I'd remain unfazed because I was so intentional about creating joy and building gratitude that there was no need for somebody else.

Even while dating, I continued my self-love practices as if no one else was there to do it for me. The second I stopped showing up for myself, the more attractive average treatment would appear to me because I wasn't gaining love anywhere else in my life. But when I buy myself flowers, hold space for my emotions, speak kindly to myself and provide all I want independently, I'm never afraid to walk away from someone I like because I'm so busy reinforcing my self-worth that their lack of reciprocation makes 'like' irrelevant.

Does it take time to find the right person? Of course, but true self-love isn't aware of how long it's taking. You don't complain that there aren't enough good men out there because your focus isn't on that, and you have enough self-belief to know that the amount of dating luck you have doesn't signify your desirability – *you* are the decider of that. In the dating phase, what you used to tolerate turns into what you refuse to negotiate. Waiting weeks for a man to ask you on a date? You've already made the reservations for a dinner date for one, put thought into the experience you want to have and made it a commitment in your calendar – if he can't match that he's no longer an option. See how much clearer red flags become when you finally put yourself on the pedestal? A lack of effort on their part becomes laughable, not something you need to question and 'wait out' just to be sure and give them a chance to act right.

This links into boundaries. When re-entering my dating life with self-love, I was unashamedly upfront about what I do and do not expect. A lot of people shy away from this out of fear they might scare somebody away, but it doesn't have to be scary. I would ask things like 'what do you think of situationships?' or mention that dating for two months without making it official was unacceptable. If they found that to be too intimidating . . . PERFECT! Then it was clear as day we don't align in our values and they were simply not meant for me.

The alternative is how I dated pre-self-love: be easy-going, don't ask for too much in the beginning (even though it's the most formative part of a relationship), go along with how they're acting and wait for them to magically get the hint on how you want to be treated. Not only is this ineffective but you're voluntarily wasting your own time. Deciding how long you want the dating phase to last and what your date requirements consist of are only the beginning of what it looks like to construct your concept of bare minimum. Like I said, this is personal for everyone, and it is substantial in determining the kind of love you receive from others. Here's an example to illustrate the differences in how you set your standards and what you receive in accordance with them:

Person A's bare minimum standards: kindness, humour, loyalty, friendship, quality time and consistent effort.

Person B's bare minimum standards: all of the above and plans weekly date nights, has emotional intelligence, ambition, self-development, aligned mindset, shared values, consistent work ethic, financial equality and support, generosity, self-care routine, meets my love language, independence, high self-esteem, regular romantic gestures, weekly flowers, compatible lifestyle goals, strong sense of self outside of the relationship, disciplined and self-controlled, loving of others, chivalrous, adventurous, open-minded, takes time to understand my personal needs, communicative, practises emotional regulation, affectionate, dates to marry, values actions over words, healthy masculine energy and supportive of my career.

Person A is more likely to risk losing out on all the standards Person B has set simply because they limited what they were looking for and are more flexible in choosing who they share their life with. When you're filled with self-love nothing is unrealistic for you. Normalise setting your non-negotiables closer to your dream ideals.

SELF-LOVE WHEN YOU ARE IN LOVE

Romantic love is an important part of your self-love journey once you've done the inner healing work. Don't make the mistake of running away from relationships and putting up a wall of hyper-independence to protect yourself from the risks of being vulnerable with another person – it will only keep you stagnant in your growth. Emotional connections and desiring love are important in your development and shutting yourself off to that experience keeps your confidence dependent on a certain set of comfortable circumstances. When you open yourself up to unpredictable situations and discomfort, this allows you to practise maintaining confidence in any environment. Allowing people to see the real you and support you through the lows elevates your self-love. It demonstrates that you have gathered such acceptance in every aspect of yourself that you can show up authentically in front of others, regardless of how it may be perceived. It doesn't matter what they may think because you've finally detached from the weight of external validation.

But this is only possible from stepping out of the safety that solitude brings and embracing the messiness that comes in building relationships. You do this by reframing your mindset – relationships, dating and friendships are no longer a matter of 'forever', but of learning instead. They are an opportunity to understand more about yourself and your triggers, and to practice higher self-esteem. Confidence adapts throughout your life and can only get stronger the more you train it – it's like a muscle, keeping self-love within the bounds of yourself doesn't test its capabilities or prepare you for when things get tough. You develop that self-love to support you in new moments of emotional stress, when you're faced with judgement, heart-break and difficult conversations, and not just in moments of normality. Other people bring out so many parts of you that can go otherwise unnoticed.

While I made significant progress in my self-perception during my year of self-love, I still made mistakes when returning to the dating world – of course I would. You will never recognise what needs to be worked on until you make the mistakes that display those unhealed parts of yourself. So much of my dating life was elevated from before but there were a few things I was trying for the first time, like casual dating and seeing multiple people at once, which brought out parts of myself I hadn't known existed.

I learned from those lessons and didn't live life in that way again because of the inner work it encouraged me to do.

When you get into a relationship, you don't leave your self-love routine behind, you keep that lifestyle the same and ensure your relationship with yourself is always number one. I balance my independence with my relationship in the following ways:

- One non-negotiable solo date and one regular date a week.
- Set a boundary for uninterrupted work/passion project hours each day and committed time each evening for quality partner time with no distractions.
- Weekly journaling to self-reflect and express gratitude and regular check-ins with partner to facilitate deeper conversations and better understanding of each other's needs.
- Monthly goal setting, calendar planning and shadow work to meet my full potential and monthly anniversary date night to set goals to grow our relationship and work on where we could improve in showing up for each other.
- Take responsibility for my own joy. Make time for hacking my happiness hormones instead of relying on my partner to feel good – he is just an addition to my life, not the centre of it.
- Have hobbies/time kept strictly for myself. For example, go to the gym alone, partner can't join in all friend time, solo date without texting throughout, and stepping outside of my comfort zone and into new environments without needing my partner to come with me.

Staying consistent in habits like these is only the start – how you honour your needs and carry yourself within the relationship is the biggest signifier of maintained relationship self-love.

Communication is a good example of this. Many people make the mistake of waiting for their partner to act right, get the hint, understand their feelings or change. Regardless of the actions of your partner, this is an unloving habit you are engaging in towards yourself. By refusing to communicate for the sake of pride and ego, you are restricting the kind of love you could be receiving. 'My partner just expects me to plan everything all the time, I'm so tired of it!' – have you explained this to them through honest and open communication? If your partner is hurting you and you feel depleted as a result, the most self-loving action you can do is to take control of the situation for your own peace of mind. Silently going along with how others treat you rather than crafting the life you desire by intentionally communicating your wants reinforces the belief that a good life can't be easy for you.

So instead, honour your needs by asking for help while remembering that other people *want* to help you and *love you* by making your life easier – you are not a burden for not being a perfect girlfriend. If you speak up when you need more attention instead of suffering in silence, you get to avoid the downward spiral of overthinking and passive aggression and replace it with getting what you want straight away because you spoke up about it. Ultimately, it's the fearlessness you hold in the possibility of being alone all over again.

Finally, being in a loving, healthy relationship is something to be proud of, but it's not your identity. You have so much more to offer as a person and there are so many more interesting aspects to know about you that being someone's girlfriend is the last piece of information you'll offer up to anybody. Your life is not supposed to revolve around your partner – and this may come as a surprise – but they're not supposed to be your number one priority. YOU are. Your future is on the pedestal, not the person. The only way to guarantee this is to continue working on your goals and growth as a top priority, not secondary to getting lost in another person's world. That way, when a possibility arises that this person may need to be removed from your life, it doesn't break you because you have an entire world you've built on your own. You have hobbies, friends, routines and fulfilment that remain even if your partner doesn't. This ensures you don't stay begging for basic decency, treatment and respect from a person who doesn't deserve you because you love the life you've built for yourself.

Self-love is not a bridge between relationships. When we experience true love from someone else, it helps us realise we're worthy of care and it heals us in many ways. Practising it while loving someone else gives you the clarity to recognise and maintain healthy love and the confidence to leave when it starts to take away from you. I value romantic love and it's always been a big life goal of mine to maintain it, but it doesn't matter how long we've been together, how many good memories there are or how much I still care for a person, the second it disturbs my self-love, I will leave without hesitation – because I love you, but I love me more.

REGULAR DATING	SELF-LOVE DATING
Constantly on the lookout for her ideal partner. Wondering where she'll meet him and how long she'll be stuck being single.	Values her singlehood and releases the need to control her dating life.
Complains about her single life and the inconvenience of her bad dating experiences.	Speaks positivity and abundance into her life through her self-belief that dating is not hard and her person will enter her life with divine timing. Unideal dating experiences are merely lessons that have shaped her standards and made her grow for the better.
Building a strategy on how to act on the first date, what to wear and when to text back.	Showing up in her authenticity confidently so she sees who is and isn't meant for her faster. After all, the only person she seeks to impress is herself.
Gets excited at a man's attractive traits, job and flirtatious conversation.	Assesses the man over time to see if his actions align with his words and how he appears on paper. Unless he adds value, there's nothing to be in awe of.

REGULAR DATING	SELF-LOVE DATING
Waits around for him to plan nicer dates, buy flowers or love her in the way she desires.	Communicates her expectations to avoid wasting her time or hurting her own feelings. She sees if the man is capable of understanding her worth and changing his actions accordingly.
Wonders why he hasn't called and why he seems so busy.	Is so busy pursuing her own hobbies and dreams that fewer texts and calls go unnoticed. Her independence and potential are her daily purpose. She doesn't have the capacity to be consumed by a relationship.

CHAPTER SUMMARY

- ☐ Seeking out validation, chasing others and placing your worth externally attracts low-value men. You become an easy target for people who add little to your life because you haven't been doing it for yourself.
- ☐ High-value men are not the prize, they are the standard. Dating with self-love is about taking it slow to assess if people are a good fit for your life after getting to know them, not falling in love with the idea of themselves that they promote.
- ☐ Giving yourself the treatment and love you crave is the easiest way to ensure you are seeking the relationship you deserve instead of jumping for joy at bare minimum effort because of your lack of familiarity with it.
- ☐ Self-love is not a bridge between relationships, it is a priority even when you're dating. The weekly solo date must continue, as will the journaling and giving love languages back to yourself along with your partner. Every time you check in with your partner to take care of them, make sure you reflect on how you've been doing and where you could improve to live a more peaceful life.
- ☐ Managing self-love when you're in love is largely about communication. Of course, this leads to a healthier relationship but it also improves the relationship and standards you have with yourself. You would never let yourself go unheard and upset through your silence. Self-love is communicating what you need so you don't

deprive yourself of the care you could receive. It also shows you the true character of your partner much sooner so you don't waste your time.

CHAPTER HOMEWORK

- ☐ Channel high-value woman energy – this has nothing to do with appearance, status and materialism, and everything to do with self-perception and confidence. Start making yourself a commitment, work on your self-sabotage, try new things to build your portfolio of proof, make self-development a priority every day through self-education and work on your inner healing via part two of this book.
- ☐ Write a list of your dream qualities in your future partner. Then write a list of your perception of bare minimum standards. Spot the gaps and combine these lists together. What you desire should be a personal non-negotiable. The closer the standards are to each other, the less you miss out on.
- ☐ Remember to maintain your own world while building alongside your partner – it is the most efficient way to embrace detachment. Don't lose yourself in the idea of another person and stay through neglect because you have nothing to go back to.

CHAPTER 12:

YOU ARE THE LOVE OF YOUR OWN LIFE

It's time to act like it

Remember that insecure relationship-reliant girl I used to be? Well, she was just as worthy of self-love as the version of myself I have now grown into. In fact, she deserved it more than ever – had I given myself that grace and attention earlier, I would have saved myself a lot of self-inflicted suffering. Having said that, the pain made me who I am today. I finally picked myself back up after years of making the same mistakes to give myself forgiveness so I could forge a new path in my life.

There was a lot of bad I could have held onto and a lot of shame I could have used to stay within the comfort of my misery, but I finally quit paying attention to my feelings and used my logic to make choices that would get me closer to the future I had always dreamed of . . . because of that one teary-eyed decision, I am where I am today – a published author, a podcaster, a businesswoman, a creator teaching over a million women to love themselves, a fulfilled and happy human being, a girlfriend finally being loved correctly and a woman who possesses so much security in herself that she makes everything her younger self could have only wished for happen in an instant.

I say this to emphasise that you don't need to have it all figured out and you certainly don't need to feel nervous about messing up on this journey – the mistakes are what make the growth so fruitful. I wouldn't have a career or anything to teach to those struggling if it wasn't for the countless trials and tribulations that provided me this knowledge. It was from the deepest points of sorrow that I made the most progress in my evolution. So, I remain thankful to the previous version of myself. Even through all her craziness and losses, she was worthy of love. The break-ups and bad decisions didn't define her – so what is there to feel guilty about? I don't sit here now feeling better about myself because I achieved my goals or got to the 'finish line' in building my self-esteem; if anything, I see even more beauty in who I used to be. She had the same heart, ambition, kindness, passion, empathy and abundant love that I have to offer now . . . so why wouldn't she be as worthy of adoration?

Having now 'mastered self-love', I don't feel nearly as finished as I once thought I would be when starting this journey. Three whole years of committed self-love later and I now know there's a lifetime of growth and love awaiting me. There's so much more to learn as I age and adapt, including parts of myself I haven't discovered because I haven't even become those versions of myself yet – how *beautiful.* Having moved on from my self-sabotaging, overly attached, unhealed days, I'm at a place in my life where I have the most solid foundation to take back the power in crafting the life best suited to me. There is no self-doubt holding me back or insecurity pushing me to hide in places that are smaller than my potential.

As wonderful as that growth is, I'm nowhere near done. I'm still pushing myself outside of my comfort zone to eradicate all possible fears – what confidence is there really if you fear anything at all? Exposure therapy is a lifelong practice. I'm saying yes without thought of the things that terrify me because letting myself overthink it is letting my past determine my future. I'm working on my communication in my relationship because my worries are simply neglected parts of me that can be soothed for while reaching safer alternatives. I'm dreaming bigger than ever because I didn't come this far just to come this far.

In a nutshell? Self-love doesn't stop with setting standards or doing your shadow work: it is an endless commitment to yourself because *you are your own soulmate.* You are the only person who can create the emotions you feel and shift the life you experience. The control was always in your own hands. It was never about the way people spoke to you or hurt you or what they could never give you – self-love was always in the way you chose yourself in those moments. Every rejection was only a path to lead you back to yourself. Every heartbreak was simply a hidden lesson in how to give yourself the love you lost.

People are additions to our lives. The only person who can complete you is yourself. You're the one who has to change the narrative, overcome the wounded parts and work to bring new abundance into your self-perception. You are the one working on filling all the little gaps you accumulated from living through your adversity; someone else can't come along to fix that for you.

Especially because we now know that no one sees you like you see you and no one has the ability to see outside of themselves. Everyone is speaking based on their own life experience, not yours . . . so how would someone else have the keys to completing what makes you, you?

This entire concept is doing everything in your capacity to provide the best for yourself – in health or activity or people, you name it – and it's when you finally step out of the version you created to feel accepted by others that you can step into a higher conscious, which puts accepting yourself first as the only priority.

We pour so much energy into teaching others how we want to be loved – but we can give ourselves our love language today.

We complain endlessly about feeling judged – but we can show up in our authenticity and confidence to feel that acceptance.

We hate the feeling of loneliness – but we can stop running from ourselves to finally feel supported.

We hate it when others misunderstand us – but when do we take time for our self-discovery?

We worry that our life is boring – but we can change the narrative and romanticise our life with a solo date.

We grow frustrated with the way we are treated – but what we tolerate is the life that we live and boundary setting is the only way up.

We wonder why we feel so sad – but we haven't been intentional in being consistent with the routines that benefit our mental health.

We hold ourselves back from pursuing our ideas – but we are

in charge of the script we write in our heads about our abilities and self-belief.

We are disturbed with memories of a traumatic past that haunt the happenings in our present – but only we can re-parent the scared inner child that is still reaching out for our understanding.

We lose ourselves when we lose someone else – but we are the loves of our own lives.

Self-love is not about distancing yourself from your flaws, it is learning how to finally embrace them in all their truth. It's key to keep this in mind as you go forth in building your new mindset. You are bound to fail and take a few steps in the wrong direction, but through it all, you are making progress. After all, you did it. You read the entire book. You now have all the information you need to flourish as you learn to love even the hardest parts of yourself. That in itself shows the commitment you have to the betterment of yourself.

Now that you know the facts, it's time to implement them – you can't feel self-love unless you're *acting* like the love of your life every single day . . . whether it's as big as a solo vacation or as small as *buying yourself the damn flowers.*

Good luck <3

ACKNOWLEDGEMENTS

There are so many people I'd like to express my thanks and gratitude for in supporting and investing in me so that I could bring the book I always needed to read to life.

To start, my grandparents. Two of the most generous people I know and the first to show me what real love feels like. Not to mention the care and patience they offered as I started writing this book in my childhood bedroom in their home. It started as a small e-book project I felt passionate about as I hoped to impart some inspiration onto other women . . . thanks to their support, I was given enough time to make it publisher pitch-worthy. Thank you for everything, Nana and Nani.

This leads me on to the team at Bonnier Books, without whom none of this would be possible. I'd like to give a special thanks for believing in me and my vision as a first-time author and in particular, my editor, Madiya Altaf, for helping me shape this into the best work possible. Without your guidance, this book truly wouldn't be the same.

It's important I highlight my wonderful agency Sixteenth, especially my manager, Kiera Pérez, who believed in me from the very start. You've shown such commitment in helping me reach my potential as a creator and in making my wildest dreams come true. From me casually mentioning my small e-book project the first time we met in a café to you passionately pitching me to various publishing houses and managing the entire process from start to finish. Thank you for all the work you do – I wouldn't have such an incredible opportunity without all your hard work and expertise.

I am also thankful for my wonderful friends who sat with me through countless café writing sessions and offered their reassurance and belief of my capabilities in creating what truly has been my most challenging piece of work to date. Thank you for your endless love and encouragement – it never goes unnoticed.

Finally, I'd like to give the biggest thanks to the wonderful women that continue to watch, like, comment and message me on social media. From the first subscribers to the millionth, every single supportive comment is held close to my heart. Throughout the process of writing, I'd read back messages and comments that detailed how my work online had resonated with my audience. After a quick re-read of these screenshotted DMs in my camera roll, I'd feel more motivated than ever. I am so grateful to have cultivated such a tight-knit community of kind, ambitious and dedicated women who are so committed to their path of self-love. It inspires me every day and I have never felt more seen or connected. It is your kindness and vulnerability in sharing your experiences and growth that encouraged me to bring this vision to life. So, I hope it helps you grow as much as it did for me . . .

ENDNOTES

Chapter 1: Everything you've been taught about self-love is incorrect

Page 15: 'If you look up self-love in the dictionary…'
Merriam-Webster Dictionary (2024). 'Self-love'. Merriam-Webster. https://www.merriam-webster.com/dictionary/self-love#:~:text=%3A%20proper%20regard%20for%20and%20attention,own%20happiness%20or%20well%2Dbeing

Page 16: 'The five love languages were identified by American author Gary Chapman in his book…'
Chapman, Gary (2015). *The Five Love Languages: How to Express Heartfelt Commitment to Your Mate*. Chicago: Moody Press.

Page 17: 'In a study done at the University of Reading…'
Weinstein, N., Vuorre, M., Adams, M. et al. (2023). 'Balance Between Solitude and Socializing: Everyday Solitude Time Both Benefits and Harms Well-Being'. Scientific Reports. 13(21160). https://doi.org/10.1038/s41598-023-44507-7

Page 20: 'Studies into the psychology behind treating yourself have shown that it helps you to regain a sense of control over your life…'
Bernecker, K., & Becker, D. (2021). 'Beyond Self-Control: Mechanisms of Hedonic Goal Pursuit and Its Relevance for Well-Being'. *Personality and Social Psychology Bulletin*. 47(4). 627-642. https://doi.org/10.1177/0146167220941998

Page 20: 'This is because touching causes the brain to release the bonding hormone oxytocin as well as relieving stress and anxiety.'
Watson, S. (2023). 'Oxytocin: The love hormone'. *Harvard Health*. https://www.health.harvard.edu/mind-and-mood/oxytocin-the-love hormone

Page 22: 'As author Mark Twain put it...'
Twain, M. 'The worst loneliness is to not be comfortable with yourself'. Goodreads. https://www.goodreads.com/quotes/83918-the-worstloneliness-is-to-not-be-comfortable-with-yourself

Page 28: 'Certified relationship coach Kate Mangona...'
Shoenthal, A. (2023). 'Three Experts on How to Set Boundaries that Actually Work'. *Forbes*. Https://www.forbes.com/sites/amyshoenthal/2023/05/26/three-experts-on-how-to-set-boundariesthat-actuallywork/#:~:text=Kate%20Mangona%20is%20a%20certified,the%20relationship%2C%E2%80%9D%20she%20says

Page 29: 'Research shows that "rates of probable mental disorders have increased since 2017. In 2020, one in six (16 per cent) children aged 5 to 16 years were identified as having a probable mental disorder"'.
NHS England (2020). 'Mental Health of Children and Young People in England, 2020: Wave 1 follow up to the 2017 survey'. *NHS Digital*. https://digital.nhs.uk/data-and-information/publications/statistical/mental-health-of-children-and-young-people-in-england/2020-wave-1-follow-up

Page 31: 'Manifestation expert Roxie Nafousi says "become aware of your inner critic..."'
Matcha Union (2021). 'Roxie Nafousi on Self-Love, Spiralling andStaying Motivated'. *Matcha Union*. https://matchaunion.com/blogs/interviews/roxie-nafousi-on-self-love-spiralling-and-staying-motivated#:~:text=The%20best%20place%20to%20start,you%20to%20build%20self%20esteem

Chapter 2: 'But I feel broken'

Page 49: 'You don't leave because trauma bonds function and holds the same power as drug addiction.'
Johnson, L. (2022). 'Trauma Bonding is as Powerful as Heroin Addiction: Why It's So Hard to Escape Toxic Relationships'. *Been There Got Out*. https://beentheregotout.com/trauma-bonding-is-as-powerful-as-heroinaddiction/

Page 56: 'Dr Shawna Freshwater PhD explains...'
Freshwater, S. (2013). 'Understanding Emotions'. *Spacious Therapy*. https://spacioustherapy.com/understanding-emotions/#:~:text=Emotions%20resonate%20with%20the%20vibrational,Life%20Force%20in%20your%20cells

Page 56: 'This scale of frequencies was originally coined by Dr David Hawkins in his book…'
Hawkins, D.R. (2020). *The Map of Consciousness Explained: A Proven Energy Scale to Actualize Your Ultimate Potential.* London: Hay House UK.

Page 57: The Emotional Vibration Frequency Chart
Smith, J. (2024). 'The Emotional Vibration Frequency Chart'. *Blisspot.* https://blisspot.com/blogs/the-emotional-vibration-analysis-frequency-chart/

Page 62: 'This concept comes from Morrie Schwartz's theory…'
Smith, A. (2023). *Morrie Schwartz's Theory of Detachment.* https://issuu.com/hhsseniorelaresearch/docs/final_perspectives_2023/s/25910810

Chapter 3: Falling off the self-love wagon

Page 77: 'Self-comparison stems from psychologist Leon Festinger's social comparison theory…'
'Social Comparison Theory'. *Psychology Today.* https://www.psychologytoday.com/gb/basics/social-comparison-theory#:~:text=According%20to%20some%20studies%2C%20as,1954%20by%20psychologist%20Leon%20Festinger

Page 80: 'This is due to a concept called arrival fallacy…'
Ben-Shahar, T. (2008). *Happier.* London: McGraw-Hill Education – Europe.

Page 92: 'Author Vex King writes in his book, *Good Vibes, Good Life*…'
King, V. (2018). *Good Vibes, Good Life.* London: Hay House UK.

Chapter 4: Tools to start your self-love journey

Page 101: 'The popular television host has said she overcame her childhood adversities by…'
Achelles, R. (2018). 'Oprah Winfrey credits her success to this one thing we all have'. *Medium.* https://medium.com/indian-thoughts/oprah-winfrey-credits-her-success-to-this-one-thing-we-all-have-4435a14b063d

Page 103: 'Psychologist Dr Juli Fraga says, "When people perceive us…"'
Morrison, C. (2023). 'Psychologist reveals the 5 signs you're a people pleaser – the personality trait that could wreak havoc on your mental health'. *MailOnline.* https://www.dailymail.co.uk/health/article-12749591/people-pleaser-trait-harms-mental-health.html

Page 120: 'As Simon Sinek states in his book…'
Sinek, S. (2011). *Start With Why*. London: Portfolio.

Chapter 5: Putting the pieces back together

Page 136: '…as explained by author Dr Robin Stern…'
Stern, R. (2007). *The Gaslight Effect*. New York: Harmony.

Page 146: 'Psychologist Dr Arielle Schwartz explains…'
Schwartz, A. (2018). *Parts Work Therapy for Complex PTSD*. Center for Resilience Informed Therapy. https://drarielleschwartz.com/parts-work-therapy-dr-arielleschwartz/#:~:text=Even%20though%20you%20are%20ready,with%20parts%20and%20ego%20states

Page 155: 'Emotional regulation is the psychological process of…'
Guy-Evans, O. (2023). 'Emotional Regulation'. *Simply Psychology*. https://www.simplypsychology.org/emotional-regulation.html

Page 161: 'According to Sigmund Freud…'
Freud S, Strachey J. (1977). *Introductory Lectures on Psychoanalysis*. New York: Norton.

Chapter 6: Transforming a break-up

Page 176: '…attachment theory, which was developed by psychologists Joel Bowlby and Mary Ainsworth…'
Bretherton I. (1992). 'The Origins of Attachment Theory: John Bowlby and Mary Ainsworth'. *Developmental Psychology* 28(5). 759-775. https://doi.org/10.1037/0012-1649.28.5.759

Page 178: 'These laws of detachment are liberating.'
Dawson, C. (2023). 'The Law of Detachment: The Beginners Guide to Emotional Freedom and Letting Go'. *Medium*. https://medium.com/@writtenbycharlotte/the-law-of-detachment-beginners-guide-to-emotional-freedom-eb75be2af24

Chapter 8: Confidence building

Page 217: 'The "looking-glass self" describes the process wherein individuals base…'
Nickerson, C. (2021). 'Looking-Glass Self: Theory, Definition & Examples'. *Simply Psychology*. https://www.simplypsychology.org/charlescooleys-looking-glass-self.html